Ken —
while a
summer ...
when I did ?, I was so
proud to see how you have
grown ... writing theology books — wow!
Peace in Emmanuel,
Fr. G. David Bline

MW01595862

THE MASS: OUR LIFE'S JOURNEY

The Mass: Our Life's Journey

Meditations and Prayers Along the Way

KENNETH W. PETERS

Preface by Adrian van Kaam, C.S.Sp., Ph.D.

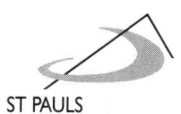

ST PAULS

Library of Congress Cataloging-in-Publication Data

Peters, Kenneth W.
    The Mass—our life's journey : meditations and prayers along the way /
by Kenneth W. Peters; preface by Adrian van Kaam.
        p. cm.
    ISBN 0-8189-1229-4
    1. Mass—Meditations. 2. Spiritual exercises.   I. Title.

BX2230.3.P47 2006
264'.02036—dc22

                        2005036429

Produced and designed in the United States of America by the
Fathers and Brothers of the Society of St. Paul,
2187 Victory Boulevard, Staten Island, New York 10314-6603,
as part of their communications apostolate.

ISBN 0-8189-1229-4
ISBN 978-0-8189-1229-0

Printing Information:

Current Printing - first digit   1   2   3   4   5   6   7   8   9   10

Year of Current Printing - first year shown

2006   2007   2008   2009   2010   2011   2012   2013   2014   2015

DEDICATION

to my wife, Ellie,
faithful partner on the spiritual journey;

to Gene Geissler, colleague and friend;

to Father Adrian van Kaam, C.S.Sp., and Dr. Susan Muto,
mentors and friends

Biblical Abbreviations

OLD TESTAMENT

Genesis	Gn	Nehemiah	Ne	Baruch	Ba
Exodus	Ex	Tobit	Tb	Ezekiel	Ezk
Leviticus	Lv	Judith	Jdt	Daniel	Dn
Numbers	Nb	Esther	Est	Hosea	Ho
Deuteronomy	Dt	1 Maccabees	1 M	Joel	Jl
Joshua	Jos	2 Maccabees	2 M	Amos	Am
Judges	Jg	Job	Jb	Obadiah	Ob
Ruth	Rt	Psalms	Ps	Jonah	Jon
1 Samuel	1 S	Proverbs	Pr	Micah	Mi
2 Samuel	2 S	Ecclesiastes	Ec	Nahum	Na
1 Kings	1 K	Song of Songs	Sg	Habakkuk	Hab
2 Kings	2 K	Wisdom	Ws	Zephaniah	Zp
1 Chronicles	1 Ch	Sirach	Si	Haggai	Hg
2 Chronicles	2 Ch	Isaiah	Is	Malachi	Ml
Ezra	Ezr	Jeremiah	Jr	Zechariah	Zc
		Lamentations	Lm		

NEW TESTAMENT

Matthew	Mt	Ephesians	Eph	Hebrews	Heb
Mark	Mk	Philippians	Ph	James	Jm
Luke	Lk	Colossians	Col	1 Peter	1 P
John	Jn	1 Thessalonians	1 Th	2 Peter	2 P
Acts	Ac	2 Thessalonians	2 Th	1 John	1 Jn
Romans	Rm	1 Timothy	1 Tm	2 John	2 Jn
1 Corinthians	1 Cor	2 Timothy	2 Tm	3 John	3 Jn
2 Corinthians	2 Cor	Titus	Tt	Jude	Jude
Galatians	Gal	Philemon	Phm	Revelation	Rv

Contents

II. The Way of Illuminative Reformation
The Following of Christ
The Liturgy of the Word

The Profession of Faith

General Intercessions: Prayer of the Faithful

III. The Way of Unifying Transformation
The Liturgy of the Eucharist: Union and Communion

The Eucharistic Prayer

Concluding Rite

IV. The Way of Contemplative Presence in the World
Dismissal

Acknowledgments

I am grateful to Eugene S. Geissler for his contribution to this book. Gene and I were co-authors of *Together at Mass* (published by Ave Maria Press in 1973). The commentaries on the prayers and parts of the Mass in that book were the inspiration for the expanded, formative renditions in *The Mass: Our Life's Journey*. Particularly notable is Gene's improvised form of the Eucharistic Prayer.

I am also particularly grateful for the gracious contribution of Father Adrian van Kaam, C.S.Sp., and Dr. Susan Muto of the Epiphany Association.

Preface

By Adrian van Kaam, C.S.Sp., Ph.D.

This book on praying and living the Mass brought me back to the pristine beginnings of the Epiphany Association in my home country, the Netherlands, in the 1930's. Our aim was to complement the doctrine and spirituality of the Church by rooting it in a detailed theory and practice of Christian formation in and through our everyday living in the midst of the world.

The center of the spiritual life of devout Christians then and now is the Holy Mass. Everyone in our prototype Epiphany group felt the need to put the Mass, with its manifold treasures of spiritual wisdom, in the center of their daily lives. They wanted to foster a meditative, spiritual reading of the Ordinary as well as the changing parts of the Mass. The meditative practice of commenting together on the prayers and scriptural readings of the day offered participants a kind of doctrinal liturgical course in Holy Scripture as read and applied by the Church in its official prayers. The participants in these group reflections developed the art and discipline of linking what they read to their own way of dwelling in the everyday world of family, commerce, study, sport, and recreation.

In this carefully crafted and inspiring work, Kenneth Peters helps us appreciate the formative power of the Mass, beginning with its introductory rites. In other meditations he presents with lucidity a commentary on my concepts of purifying formation, illuminating reformation, and unifying transformation. He relates these stages of graced unfolding to each phase of the Mass. His salient remarks merit our fullest attention, for liturgy, word, and sacrament are at the heart of our Christian spiritual life.

Already in pre-war Holland we witnessed the first signs not only of a hunger for spiritual experience but a growing inclination in some people to detach spirituality from the great religious and ecclesial traditions that were their very foundation. Later these increasing attempts to devise a separate non-ecclesial spirituality gave rise to so-called new age spirituality.

At present such trends have attained great popularity, but they exist loosened from solid faith traditions and teachings of the Church. This popularity is witnessed by the immense sales of non-traditional or non-ecclesial books on a variety of transpersonal approaches. Books on "spirit" are being published in overwhelming numbers today.

To celebrate the Eucharist is to give ecclesial form to our life. It is to experience deeper intimacy with Christ in a common yet unique way. It is to experience a firm grounding in the rich treasures of our faith and formation tradition.

The author's meditations and prayers facilitate our return to this original center. We hope and pray that many believers tainted unwittingly by certain attractive tenets of popular transpersonal movements may become sensitive to the form-traditional or traditionally formative spirituality* from which their life in Christ should originate and to which it should return.

---

* Co-founded by Father Adrian and Dr. Susan Muto in Pittsburgh in 1979, the present Epiphany Association has as one of its major aims to make clear to members around the world the stand for a "form-traditional spirituality," rooted in a basic religious or ecclesial tradition, that helps us to bring together what we believe and how we live. The phrase "formative spirituality" is Father Adrian's way to identify in shorthand form the fuller theme of "ecclesial-experiential, form traditional spirituality."

Foreword

Is the Eucharist the source and center of my life? of your life?

For over 2,000 years now since the Last Supper in the Upper Room in Jerusalem, the spiritual formation of the people of God, the laity, happened through the recalling and living out their baptismal commitment in the Mass, the Paschal Mystery. For generations the piety of Catholics, and increasingly that of other Christians with liturgical traditions, has been nourished by this outstanding weekly, if not daily, event and celebration. The missals that old-timers carried back and forth to Mass and often used at home were a mark of the times, as well as a source of continuing inspiration and education. Today, in large part, the missals are gone, though the need for inspiration and education remains.

Since Vatican II, the use of English and other liturgical changes have enabled the people to "hear" and understand the prayers of the Mass and to "listen" to the proclamation of the word of God. The direct relationship between priest and people in community has helped to mold the people of God more closely together in celebration. Yet, with all the renewal of the liturgy, little attention has been given to its potential to form (*not merely inform*) people in their lives of prayer and their own individual spiritual journeys and to have that faith in action take form in their everyday lives. We need some attention to the spirituality of the Mass to express this unique Christian assembly — an assembly brought together and made one by the body and blood and heartbeat of Jesus, and by the Spirit of Christ active among God's people.

Introduction: Why the Mass?

"Do this in memory of me."

When the apostles gathered with Jesus in the upper room to celebrate the Passover, they could not have known the entire significance of what they were about. They did know that they met as friends, in the warm and intimate setting of a meal, with one who loved them and whom they had come to love.

There was ritual, indeed, and some realization that this was no ordinary meal, but what would remain with them long after their hunger was satisfied and the ritual performed was the reality of what Jesus said and did, and the sense of a new relationship with him and with one another. They had experienced Eucharist.

They had also experienced in prophecy what the *Catechism of the Catholic Church* aptly sums up as follows:

> At the Last Supper, on the night he was betrayed, our Savior instituted the Eucharistic sacrifice of his Body and Blood. This he did in order to perpetuate the sacrifice of the cross throughout the ages until he should come again, and so to entrust to his beloved Spouse, the Church, a memorial of his death and resurrection: a sacrament of love, a sign of unity, a bond of charity, a Paschal banquet "in which Christ is con-

sumed, the mind is filled with grace, and a pledge of future glory is given to us" (*Sacrosanctum concilium* 47).

Is this what we Catholics experience in attending Mass today? True we may have heard from childhood that the Mass is the central act of the Christian life. We may know the liturgical expressions in which the act of worship is cast: Introductory Rites, Liturgy of the Word, Liturgy of the Eucharist, Rite of Communion, Concluding Rites. But many of us, if we are to judge by appearances and by our own admission, fail to experience on a personal level what the Mass should be. Do we really experience ourselves as a worshiping community, a gathering in Christ? Are we aware as we might be of Christ's loving sacrifice being renewed in our lives?

If we are not so aware, would we not appreciate an approach to the Mass that is sensitive to our deepest needs as human beings — needs that can be filled only by the Spirit of God? If we are to give credibility to our claim to be created "in the image and likeness of God" and to be conformed to the likeness of God's Son, would it not be useful for us to reflect on our dignity and how to maintain it? How can we gaze into this mirror of likeness?

Spiritual Formation: The Three Ways

In this book the meditations on the prayers and liturgical actions of the Mass present a program of spiritual formation founded on the traditional "ways" of the spiritual journey, namely, "the purgative way," "the illuminative way," and "the unitive way." These three ways or stages on the journey have guided hosts of serious Christians for ages in their search for a closer union with God. They can illustrate in a convincing manner a "formation program" for us, to guide us in our understanding and pursuit of the art and practice of living out what we believe in everyday life. This is important in our day when the search for "spiritual experience" is rampant, often manifesting itself in bizarre and ineffective ways.

The three ways of the spiritual journey can help us to understand what it means to live a spiritual life, one guided and sustained by the Spirit of God. We know that our lives as Christians must be lives of continual conversion. Having come from God, we are destined to return to God in spite of many obstacles along the way. To "convert" means *to turn away from* anything that would keep us from that return and *to turn toward* the only way back. Anyone who has witnessed a baptism today knows that conversion means a turning away from all the disorder we have inherited from "the sin of the world," as well as from our own personal sinfulness. Conversion is a lifelong task of turning away from the deformative path of sin and turning toward Jesus Christ, the one who saves us. It is the way of purification, illumination, and union.

Traveling this way can also be an experience of ordering our lives so as to form a human and Christian character and personality, the image of Jesus in us destined for each of us by the Father from all eternity. It is the way of a holistic Christian humanism, if you will. Unlike the passing nature of an "awakening experience," the spiritual journey is a lifetime project, not a quick fix. It is a way of finding and following the will of God. And, not incidentally, it is medicine for the sickness in our world today.

Considering "the many problems [that] darken the horizons of our time," the late Pope John Paul II quotes St. Ignatius of Antioch who "rightly defined the Eucharistic bread as 'a medicine of immortality, an antidote to death.'" On the world's many problems, the Pope writes:

We need but think of the urgent need to work for peace, to base relationships between peoples on solid premises of justice and solidarity, and to defend human life from conception to its natural end. And what should we say of the thousand inconsistencies of a "globalized" world where the weakest, the most powerless and the poorest appear to have so little hope! It is in this world that Christian hope must shine forth! For this reason too, the Lord wished to remain with us in the Eucharist, making his presence in meal and sacrifice the promise of a humanity renewed by his love.   (*On the Eucharist in Its Relationship to the Church*, chapter one, "The Mystery of Faith").

In this task of sharing the spiritual wisdom of the ages, we will rely heavily on the spirit and work of Father Adrian van Kaam, C.S.Sp., and Dr. Susan Muto, founder and collaborator, respectively, of the discipline and practice of formative spirituality. Father van Kaam's threefold path of spiritual deepening, namely, "purifying formation, illuminative reformation, and unifying transformation,"[1] puts in formative perspective the aforementioned three traditional facets of the spiritual journey: the purgative, illuminative, and unitive ways.

For our purposes in relation to the Mass, we name these three traditional paths: The Way of Purifying Formation, The Way of Illuminative Reformation (The Following of Christ), and The Way of Transforming Union. The result of a faithful living out of this spiritual journey is the formation of Christian character, designated here as "The Way of Contemplative Presence," the life of the Trinity in thought and action in the world. The

---

[1] Cf. Adrian van Kaam, *Transcendent Formation, Formation Spirituality*, Volume VI.

spiritual experience of this traditional spiritual journey is an awesome possibility as we live the Mass. Reflection and prayer will help us make it real.

The foregoing process is the way of partnership with God, a cooperation in God's work in us and in the world today. The meditations and prayers relating the Mass to the spiritual journey are outlined as follows:

1. In the Introductory Rites, we pilgrims on the spiritual journey go through a *purifying formation. We* repent of our sins and faults; *God* purifies us. Our theme: "Create a clean heart in me, O God!" (Ps 51).

2. In the Liturgy of the Word, we are enlightened in the way of the imitation and following of Christ, the way of *illuminative reformation. We* come to Jesus; *Jesus* instructs and accompanies us. Our theme: "I am the light of the world" (Jn 8:12). "Come to me all you who are weary and find life burdensome, and I will refresh you…. Learn from me, for I am gentle and humble of heart" (Mt 11:28, 29).

3. In the Liturgy of the Eucharist, we are invited to the banquet of *unifying transformation. We* surrender in faith and trust; the *Trinity* deepens its life in us. Our theme: "Anyone who loves me will be true to my word, and my Father will love them; we will come to them and make our home with them" (Jn 14:23).

4. We are sent out from the Mass to be a *"contemplative presence* in the world," an instrument of service for our own salvation and that of our neighbor, salvation founded on the light and life of Christ within us. Our theme: "Go, the Mass is ended. Go to love and serve God and one another."

This is a book of meditations, not a book to be simply read through. We invite you to make this account of your spiritual journey one of prayer and personal expression, perhaps in a journal. Use it before the Blessed Sacrament, or in your prayer or discussion group.

PRAYER

I am so needy, Lord, only you know how much. But your Spirit speaks in me with "unutterable groanings" for the things I really need. Why do I go to Mass? Do I really believe and experience the action of your Holy Spirit in my life when I assist at Mass? Help me to accept your ministering to me, your direction and nourishment in my life.

Come, Holy Spirit, enlighten my mind and stir my heart. Help me to understand your great mercy and love in continuing your word and your presence in the people of God and in the world through the Mass. Guide me in this spiritual journey as I contemplate the gift of the Mass in my life.

Let the journey begin!

Our forebears in the Jewish faith celebrated their Passover, their freedom (*their purification*) from the slavery of sin and subjection in Egypt through 40 years in the desert, to finally enter into the Promised Land. We celebrate our passover in Christ's sacrifice for our sins, for our continued formation in his teachings and life, and our eventual entrance into the promised land of everlasting life. It is Jesus Christ who is our Pasch, the pure sacrificial lamb, the "scapegoat" for our sins, who, "gentle and humble of heart," was led to his death, and who frees us from sin and death.

Unless we forget, the Mass is celebrated throughout the world "that sins might be forgiven." The Eucharistic mystery, stripped of its sacrificial meaning [writes Pope John Paul in the encyclical cited above], is celebrated as if it were simply a fraternal banquet. Furthermore, the necessity of the ministerial priesthood, grounded in apostolic succession, is at times obscured and the sacramental nature of the Eucharist is reduced to its mere effectiveness as a form of proclamation.

How does it happen that we are freed from sin and death? As we know, life is not a bed of roses. In our better moments, however, we experience life's limitless gifts. Scripture, as well as our own experience, tells us that God intends for us to live lives of peace and joy in God's love. It is an awesome fact that we have been in the mind and heart of God, a place of paradisal peace and joy, from before we were born. This is incredibly good news. The Book of Proverbs poetically pictures the Word of God during the creation of the universe: "Playing before him all the while, playing on the surface of the earth. And I found delight in the children of men" (8:30-31).

Unfortunately, sin entered the picture, our own rebellion shown first in Adam, the biblical name for "humankind." Fortunately, Romans says, as sin entered our world through one man, so grace entered even more copiously through one man, Jesus Christ. Jesus, God incarnate, then becomes the pattern for our own formation in grace, the original image in which we were formed in the likeness of God. God still delights in his children!

Formation spirituality expresses this basic truth about life, namely, that we — our bodies and physical and mental abilities, and eventually our characters and personalities — are continually being formed and shaped. This is vividly expressed in Psalm 139: "For thou didst *form* my inward parts, thou didst knit me together in my mother's womb. I praise thee, for I am fearfully and wonderfully made!" (vs. 13-14). As we are formed, we are also being *reformed* through our Christian life and, through grace, we trust, ultimately *transformed*. This is our awesome beginning and our predestined end: beginning from our Source, the heart and mind of our loving God, we are on our journey back to unity with the Trinity. What an awesome destiny!

PRAYER

Lord, let me enter into this process of conversion, the ways of purifying formation, of illuminative reformation, and of transforming union. You have planned this journey from all eternity especially for me, especially for each of your children. Let me not miss the mark.

THE MASS: OUR LIFE'S JOURNEY
Meditations and Prayers Along the Way

The Eucharist is "the source and summit of the Christian life."
(LG 11)

"It remains the center of the Church's life."
(Catechism of the Catholic Church, 1343)

I

The Way of Purifying Formation

"Create in me a clean heart, O God."
(Ps 51)

INTRODUCTORY RITES

1. Come Celebrate Christ!

There is no Mass, much less a "celebration" of Mass — to say nothing of any remedy for sin and hope for purification and salvation — without Jesus Christ. It is he who gathers us together; it is he who is our sacrifice; it is he who binds us into one; it is he who is both present and becomes present again; it is he who moves among us and gives meaning not only to our individual lives, but also to our coming together as his people; it is he who is our past, present, and future because he is yesterday, today, and forever.

In a very real sense, the Church celebrates the whole life, death, and resurrection mystery of Christ every time she assembles for Mass. Jesus joined the human race and lives our human life. He is the ever-revealing Word of God. He is the only one who has gone before us through living, suffering, and dying to be raised up. He is the one seated at the right hand of the Father who intercedes for us. It is he who sends his Spirit upon us.

The Spirit of Jesus is alive and active in the Introductory Rites as well as in the Liturgy of the Word and the Liturgy of the Eucharist. All is creative in building up the people of God. We learn once again to listen to the word of God calling us to repentance, because it is a living word different from all other words. We listen to each other in the confession of our sinfulness, for we are "little words" in the divine Word. "In the beginning was the Word, and the Word was with God, and the Word was God" (Jn 1:1). Jesus Christ, we know, is the Word made flesh.

It is true, the Word made flesh is not the same as the "words

3

of God" in the Bible, or more especially in us as "little words." Nevertheless, all is closely related, all is God's presence. Through the words of the Bible we meet Jesus Christ, the one Word God has spoken, and we meet each other in Christ. He is the living Word who does his work in each of us as we listen.

PRAYER

Jesus, you are the Word of God who became flesh to live among us. Because I am on my way back to God along with you, your story has become my story. Lead me, guide me along the way of my spiritual journey, for "You have created me for yourself alone, and my heart is restless until it rests in you" (St. Augustine).

2. Entrance Song and Greeting

Why have we come together? Surely one reason is that we need one another. But, most of all, we need Christ. If living has taught us anything, it is that acceptance, forgiveness, love, joy — the lack of which comes from our inability to respond in love to a loving God, resulting in sin and sadness — do not come except through people who have been graced with God's love in Jesus Christ.

But why gather for Mass, for worship? Do not the family dinner, the get-together with friends, the sharing of our everyday lives, each in its own way, serve the need for reconciliation and for our being with and sharing love with others? Indeed, they do.

But where is the gathering that satisfies the deepest and most universal need in the hearts of all to be accepted (and to accept), to be forgiven (and to forgive), to be loved (and to love)

— to be one, and to celebrate that oneness? Where is the ultimate gathering where all human beings can offer that reconciliation with God and with one another in one perfect sacrifice?

> When the Church celebrates the Eucharist, the memorial of her Lord's death and resurrection, this central event of salvation becomes really present and "the work of our redemption is carried out." This sacrifice is so decisive for the salvation of the human race that Jesus Christ offered it and returned to the Father only *after he had left us a means of sharing in it* as if we had been present there. Each member of the faithful can thus take part in it and inexhaustibly gain its fruits.
> (John Paul II, Encyclical, *On the Eucharist in Its Relationship to the Church,* chapter one, "The Mystery of Faith")

The Mass, then, our faith tells us, is the ultimate gathering in Christ, the perfect sacrifice. In the Mass is Christ, the touchstone, the foundation of all wholeness — human and divine. His word, his offering, his power, his redeeming, cross-bearing-unto-death love are there in a special way, under effective signs of reconciliation.

In our time when sister is separated from sister, and brother from brother, not only many times by physical miles but spiritual light-years, we need a gathering where all can come together in peace and love — in yearning, if not yet in fact.

So we gather at Mass, from all over the neighborhood, and from the ends of the earth. We come together greeting one another. (How can we love one another if we do not acknowledge each other?) One way to greet another is with a smile, or a nod. We join in the entrance song with full voice and earnest joy, opening ourselves and making ourselves vulnerable (especially should our song be less than perfect). Our senses, our very humanness, even our openness to admit our sins and faults, express the desire of our spirit to offer all that we are, all that we have, and all that we can be in union with Christ and our fellow human beings.

PRAYER

Cry out with joy to the Lord, all the earth.
Serve the Lord with gladness.
Come before him, singing for joy (Ps 100).

My heart is bursting with the sights and sounds of your goodness, O Lord. How can I hold it inside, and not give you praise?

3. Call to Worship

We are *religious beings*. By divine dispensation we are bound to God, in spite of our creaturehood and our sinfulness. Human beings have need to worship. We are more than mere creatures; we are "made in the image and likeness of God" and have an inborn dynamic for the transcendent, for seeking that which is above. Human beings recognize their Creator and worship that Supreme Being. It is essential that we worship God rather than something else — our own self, our passions, our possessions, our achievements.

We are *social beings*. Humans have need to worship together with others. We interact with each other, we influence one another, we help to form each other. In the words of formation spirituality, we are agents of each other's "formation."[2] So we

---

[2] Terms in quotes are, in general, taken from Adrian van Kaam's works on Formation Spirituality.

come together in church, a sacred place, a place made sacred by our coming together for worship.

We are the *people of God*. We come as consecrated people. We are people for *all* people, for those who have come and those who haven't — those who have come for worship *for* (on behalf of) those who haven't. It will always be that way because we represent one another before the Lord.

And when we do, we are "salt of the earth!" We are the "light of the world!" We are "a royal priesthood!"

From among the people one has been set aside and ordained to lead in worship. He joins them and greets them. His greeting is a call to worship. With him we say: "Come, let us worship the Lord; for he is our God and we are his people."

PRAYER

Lord, it is difficult for me to believe that I am "salt," "light," member of a "royal priesthood," but it is not I who have named me thus. Make me worthy to offer your sacrifice, and my sacrifice, for the life of the world.

PENITENTIAL RITE

"Create a clean heart in me, O God!"
*"My brothers and sisters, to prepare ourselves to celebrate
the sacred mysteries, let us call to mind our sins."*

4. Recalling Our Sinfulness

People have a need to be "saved," to know that in spite of their sometimes twisted and unruly lives, they are accepted and forgiven. Yet, we are reluctant to talk about sin today.

St. James in his epistle asserts that there is no truth (and no peace) in us who say that we are without sin. The evidence is all around us: the unkind remark that cuts, the flush that comes when we push anger too far, the prejudice that reddens our faces, our damaged pride, the urge to strike back, our self-righteous stand, to say nothing of compulsive living, consumer addiction, mental, emotional, and physical violence. How often do we not feel the disorder of sin in our very bones? How often must we say with the apostle Paul: "The evil that I would not, that I do"?

That evil extends much farther than our individual persons into family strife, civic disorder, racism, war. This personal and social experience of sin — and along with perhaps its mildest manifestation, the so-called "low-grade depression" — shows itself in such alarming numbers in our materialistic and functionalistic world, where all is geared toward production and accomplishment to feed our voracious appetites for the "good life," a situation which often yields such sad returns. The whole world, it seems, is in a kind of "dark night" of pain, anxiety, and grief which is "our unique and universal reality. It is a description of our world, our neighborhood, our family life."[3]

---

[3] Susan Muto, *John of the Cross Today: The Dark Night.* Ave Maria Press, Notre Dame, IN, 1994, p. 18.

This "sin sickness" infests Christians also, in our work, in our families, and in our parishes. How many people today are in a spiritual wasteland, in a kind of "dark night" of their own, of which they know no way out?

There is a remedy for this cancerous running on. God loved us "even when we were in sin," and God has accepted and forgiven us. God has forgiven us, especially in Jesus. We can be purged of our addictions. "Here is a saying that you can rely on and nobody should doubt," Paul assures us: "Christ Jesus came into the world to save sinners." We are at Mass precisely to acknowledge this tremendous goodness of our God, to celebrate it, to make ourselves ever more aware of it in order to participate in it more fully. But we ought first to admit our sin.

The gospel suggests that if we have anything against our brother or sister we ought first to go and reconcile ourselves with them, and then come and offer our gift. At least let us recall our faults, repent of them, and renew our resolve to love our brothers and sisters: spouse, children, next door neighbor, fellow worker, relatives and friends, the poor, our enemies, the unwanted, sinners, the forgotten of this world.

Then, let us ask for mercy.

PRAYER

Lord, you call me to remember my sins, not for any guilt trip of my own, but for me to experience your gracious forgiveness. How can I know where I need healing, if you do not show me my wounds? Treat me gently, Lord!

5. "Let Us Call to Mind Our Sins"

If we wish to "call to mind our sins," as the celebrant invites us to in the Mass, we will probably not find a better way than to meditate on Psalm 51. Listen to the Psalmist's description of the way of real repentance and purification:

Have mercy on me, O God, in your goodness;
in the greatness of your compassion wipe out my offense.
Thoroughly wash me from my guilt
and of my sins cleanse me.
For I acknowledge my offense,
and my sin is before me always:
Against you only have I sinned,
and done what is evil in your sight (vs. 3-6).

It is against the goodness and loving kindness of our God that we have sinned, not only against our own selves or other human beings. God, then, is the principal one who can forgive us and purify us. In his compassion, God in Jesus, who is "like us in all things except sin," suffers with us. But we need to acknowledge our sin and, as it were, have it "before us always."

Unfortunately, as we have seen, we are the victims of "original" sin and of our own sin sickness. "Indeed, in guilt was I born, and in sin my mother conceived me" (Ps 51:7). With clouded spirits and the tendency we have to excuse ourselves, we often do not know our sin — that is, admit that our experience of it is what is hurting us — enough to acknowledge it. Yet, how much of the violence in our world today — domestic and civic — is due to unacknowledged and unrepented sin. "Whatever happened to sin?" asked the title of a book by psychiatrist Karl Menninger. We do not talk about sin in our therapeutic society today. Do we really know what our real sin is, and from whence it arises?

As we are being *formed*, and help to form each other, as previously noted, we can also be *deformed*, misled, twisted, and caught in inept and damaging ways of "the world, the flesh, and the devil," what spiritual masters have called the result of that same original sin. We are deformed through our own and others' sins and faults. All of us, in some way, have felt the sting of the all-pervasive poison of rebellion against God. Perhaps in our personal examination of conscience, we might do well to examine whole areas of sin in our lives, as well as particular acts of anger, hate, and lust, in order to know what our real sin is and from where it comes.

What is the spiritual atmosphere most conducive to this personal formative inquiry about sin? Again, Psalm 51:

> Behold, you are pleased with sincerity of heart,
> and in my inmost being you teach me wisdom....
> A clean heart create for me, O God,
> and a steadfast spirit renew within me.
> Cast me not out from your presence,
> and your holy spirit take not from me (vs. 12-13).

PRAYER

O God of mercy, in the secret of my heart, when I am not entirely at peace with you and my neighbor, reveal to me my real sin. A clean heart create in me, O Lord. A steadfast spirit renew within me.

6. A Personal Inventory

For some of us, perhaps, the "examination of conscience" conjures up thoughts of troubled experiences of confession in the past. That should not be the experience of today's sacrament of Reconciliation. We should not forget, however, that Christ's sacrifice is the principal source of forgiveness and reconciliation. The Church prescribes confession in the sacrament of Reconciliation for "mortal sin" so that we might receive the grace of the Eucharist effectively.

To say that we have a remedy for sin in the Eucharist, however, is not to downgrade the sacrament of Reconciliation. This sacrament, as all the sacraments, is oriented toward the sacrament of the Eucharist and shares its power. "These two sacraments are very closely connected," writes Pope John Paul II in his encyclical *On the Eucharist...*:

Because the Eucharist makes present the redeeming sacrifice of the cross, perpetuating it sacramentally, it naturally gives rise to a continuous need for conversion, for a personal response to the appeal made by Saint Paul to the Christians of Corinth: "We beseech you on behalf of Christ, be reconciled to God" (2 Cor 5:20). If a Christian's conscience is burdened by serious sin, then that path of penance through the sacrament of Reconciliation becomes necessary for full participation in the Eucharistic Sacrifice (Chapter 4).

The Psalmist prays not to be "cast out" of God's loving presence and the grace of the Holy Spirit because of our sin.

Not knowing how to examine ourselves, we can unwittingly follow a sterile, if not dangerous, path leading us to scrutinize our sinful selves in an overly introspective way, without the moderating and benevolent "presence" of the loving and forgiving God. It is not God who casts us out of that presence, just as God does not take his Spirit from us. It is we who hide ourselves, as Adam and Eve did in the garden when they found out they were naked after they had sinned.

Van Kaam calls the way of seeing ourselves in the Presence, the light and warmth and forgiveness, of our benevolent God, "transcendent self-presence." Here, with all our warts, we look at ourselves "with sincerity of heart" as our compassionate God sees us. In that environment, God can teach us wisdom "in our inmost being" — wisdom that enviable quality that comes from the experience of knowing how to implement the directives that God has planned for our lives according to his love.[4] We see what we have done wrong in humility and good heart, and we are counseled how to repair the damage to ourselves and others, along with the consolation of God: "A contrite and humble heart, you will not scorn" (Ps 51:19). It is, after all, God who calls us to repentance, along with our troubled consciences. God will not be outdone in generous forgiveness.

PRAYER

Along with a clean heart, O God, give me a heart that is contrite and humble. It is because of your overwhelming mercy and love, that I am able to express my sorrow and to accept your forgiveness. You do treat me gently, Lord.

---

[4] Cf. van Kaam's constructs of transcendent self-presence and the love-will of God in our behalf in his works on Formation Spirituality.

7. Sin: Who Gets Hurt?

"As long as nobody gets hurt...," we might hear someone say. Who gets hurt when we sin? With our most secret excesses, our secret addictions, our secret self-seeking, we certainly hurt ourselves. We continue the deformation begun in Adam. Even though our sins might not be visible, someone besides ourselves always gets hurt. Our community is deformed. We are limited creatures. What we do for our own self-interest, we may deny another. Perhaps we do not harm the person with whom we are directly involved — our spouses, our children, our fellow workers — but we poison the spiritual atmosphere with ill-conceived motives and plans. We may not think we are hurting these others, only to discover later with a bit of sincere reflection that we did just that.

So, "Forgive us as we forgive each other," the Lord has taught us. We are sinners, we sin all the time. Somebody is always getting hurt in some way. By our sins we are deforming ourselves and our neighbors.

"I confess to... God, and to you my brothers and sisters...." To confess to God is already to be forgiven. A brother or sister's hurts, however, are not always healed that easily.

Therefore, we pray together to be healed and reconciled with our brothers and sisters, our relatives, our friends so that we might be reconciled with God.

Jesus, of course, presents the program and the model for the change of heart necessary for real repentance and forgiveness. Jesus' message at the beginning of his ministry announcing the kingdom was, "Repent and believe in the Good News."

> The kingdom of God announced by Christ [wrote Pope Paul VI], can be entered only by a "change of heart" (metanoia), that is to say, through that intimate

and total change and renewal of the entire person — of all of one's opinions, judgments and decisions — which takes place in us in the light of the sanctity and charity of God, the sanctity and charity which were manifested to us in the Son and communicated fully.

The invitation of the Son to "metanoia" becomes all the more inescapable inasmuch as he not only preaches it but himself offers an example. Christ, in fact, is the supreme model for those doing penance. He willed to suffer punishment for sins which were not his but those of others ("Poenitemini," 1966).

PRAYER

O God, I would do well to reflect often on Pope Paul's words on repentance and on Jesus' good news. In the secret of my heart teach me wisdom that I may answer the invitation of Jesus to change my heart and enter his kingdom of love and forgiveness.

8. Love of Enemies

We are not finished with reconciliation with those near and dear to us. The Lord, it seems, had more in mind. We must also love those who do not love us.

"Love your enemies," Jesus said, "pray for those who persecute you.... This will prove that you are sons and daughters of your heavenly Father. For his sun rises on the bad and on the good, he rains on the just and the unjust. If you love those who love you, what merit is there in that? Do not the [hated] tax collectors do as much? … In a word, you must be made perfect as your heavenly Father is perfect" (See Mt 5:43-48).

Does that seem impossible? Notice that Jesus says *you must be made perfect.* This is indeed impossible for unaided human nature, but Jesus tells us also, "Nothing is impossible with God." Many, many years ago, in the heat of the civil rights struggle, there was a title of a book by James Forest, *Making Friends of Enemies.* Christians ought not to have "enemies." The best way to make enemies into friends is to pray for them, and to act toward them as you would have them act toward you. In fact, that is a good test for a Christian.

"Be made perfect as your heavenly Father is perfect." Scripture tells us more about the "how":

> Be compassionate as your Father is compassionate. Do not judge, and you will not be condemned. Pardon, and you shall be pardoned. Give, and it shall be given to you. Good measure pressed down, shaken together, running over, will pour into the fold of your garment. For the measure you measure with will be measured back to you (Lk 6:36-38).

God will not be outdone in generosity.

PRAYER

Who are my enemies, Lord? Your words about compassion and not judging cut my heart to the quick. Help me, Lord! Of myself it seems an impossible task but you promise that nothing is impossible with you.

9. Forgiveness and Compassion

Why is forgiveness so crucial?

The biblical notion of sin can give us a clue to answering this question. Sin in Scripture is "missing the mark," a deformation caused by our lack of coming up to the design God has for our lives. In that sense, we [even "the just man"] sin, as Scripture has it, at least seven times a day, often unwittingly. Jesus, therefore, says "Forgive not seven times, but seventy times seven times," that is, as many times as needed.

Forgiveness of, and compassion for, enemies, yes — but also for our family members, our working relationships, our friends, anyone who has hurt us and whom we have hurt. Is it perhaps not sometimes easier to forgive enemies than to forgive friends? Yet, modern psychology tells us that lack of forgiveness on our part is the source of much of our misery — in families, in the workplace, in all kinds of relationships.

Listen again to Pope Paul VI on forgiveness, in his Ash Wednesday message in 1986:

> Without any doubt, many quarrels and disputes come to an end through a simple effort of good will. These reconciliations have a great educative and spiritual value — for those who bring them about, for those who benefit from them, and for those who witness them.
>
> And so, far from neglecting these little daily reconciliations, we ought to increase their number: they form, as it were, the thread of the fabric of society. Is it not true to say that life in common — married life, family life, life in community, business life, city life, the nation's life — is a continuous succession of quar-

rels overcome and even forgiven as many as 'seventy times seven' times? (cf. Mt 18:22).

Jesus in his great homily in the Sermon on the Mount advises us that if we do not forgive others, God will not be able to forgive us. A weighty and awesome statement! But, listen to reason: how can God forgive us if we continue to harbor hatred in our hearts? Not to forgive others is not to experience forgiveness in our own spirit. Ask anyone who has had either experience.

God so desires this experience for us. Reflect on the prayer the Church says every morning in the Liturgy of the Hours, the Canticle of Zechariah. It would be good to meditate on this passage before coming to Mass.

Blessed be the Lord the God of Israel because
    he has come to his people and set them free.
He has raised up for us a mighty savior,
    born of the house of his servant David.

We have been told this "good news" by the Church from the time of our birth from our mother's womb: God has visited — and become one of us — through Jesus who still lives among us. Why?

To set us free from the hands of our enemies,
    free to worship him without fear,
holy and righteous in his sight
    all the days of our life....
to give his people knowledge of salvation
    by the forgiveness of their sins (italics mine).

What a promise: to free us from our "enemies," our sins, through repentance. Freedom from fear, from the destructive pattern of deformation and ruined relationships, through the "knowledge of salvation by the forgiveness of our sins." Therefore, let us call for mercy from our merciful God!

PRAYER

Kyrie Eleison, Lord, have mercy.
Christe Eleison, Christ, have mercy.
Kyrie Eleison, Lord, have mercy.

10. We Call for Mercy

You were sent to heal the contrite: Lord, have mercy.
You came to call sinners: Christ, have mercy.
You plead for us at the right hand of the Father: Lord, have mercy.
The final verses of the Canticle of Zechariah are the most reassuring and comforting:

In the tender compassion of our God
the dawn from on high shall break upon us,
to shine on those who dwell in darkness
and the shadow of death,
and to guide our feet into the way of peace.

God has compassion for us, that is, he "suffers with" us. An interpreter of Scripture suggests that God suffers in his desire for our happiness, in his very "guts," if we may so vulgarize it. In his compassion he sends his "dawn from on high." "All this is the work of the kindness of our God, he, the Dayspring, shall visit us in his mercy," another translation has it. Jesus shines in the darkness for us in the shadow of death in order to guide our feet into the way of peace. Is that not what, in our deep spirits, we most desire?

PRAYER

Lord, "from my secret sins, cleanse me." Lord Jesus, you came to save me, a sinner, so that I, a sinner, might help to save others — even my enemies — by doing them good. You are a loving, just, merciful, and saving Lord!

GLORIA

"Glory to God in the highest, and peace to his people on earth."

11. We Praise God

Having repented of our sins and failings, we are ready to give glory to God. We praise God. We thank him. Certainly not for any need that God might have, but for the need we have. A glowing sunset, the majesty of a mountain, the touch of an infant's hand... these signs of God move even the most insensitive of us. There is such beauty and goodness in the world that God created, both in nature and in grace, that reflection on it practically forces a response. If we are silent, Jesus tells us, "The very stones will cry out!"

Therefore, here at the beginning of Mass, we appropriately praise and thank God and call down peace upon God's people.

We praise our *Father Creator* for his creation and for having revealed to us his mercy and love. At the birth of his Son Jesus, the angels sang: "Glory to God in the highest, and peace to those who enjoy God's favor." The favor God has shown to us is his grace freely given in Jesus. From our baptism we all enjoy God's favor.

We thank the *Son* for taking away our sins. He is the lamb of God who was sacrificed for us. He is the reason we can, in the words of Romans, "Offer ourselves as living sacrifices, holy and pleasing to God, your spiritual worship" (12:1). He is "seated at the right hand of the Father," and he receives our prayer. For he alone is the "Holy One," he alone is the "Lord," he alone is the "Most High."

We court the *Spirit* for Jesus' continuing presence among us. From the time of creation, when the Spirit "hovered over the waters," through the Spirit's presence with the Chosen People, that same Spirit comes down upon us in the sacraments, in water, blood, and fire. We expect great things to come.

We look around at our neighbors and remind ourselves that, as the folk song has it, "Everything's beautiful in its own way," because every thing and every person is a reflection of God. Look around you, and find many reasons to praise and thank God.

PRAYER

Lord, take the cloud away from my dull perception, open my eyes and my ears to the beauty all around me. Forgive me for being negative about your world and the people you have created. Help me always to have great expectations. Thank you, Father, Son, and Holy Spirit! Glory to God in the highest and peace to his people on earth.

12. The Goodness of God

Because God first loved us, we exist, and God loves us once and for all. Whether we love God or not, God loves us. God's name is love. "God is love, and he who abides in love abides in God and God in him" (1 Jn 3:16).

But we *do* love God, for to know God is to love God, and he has made it possible to love him. "We, for our part, love because he first loved us" (1 Jn 3:19). Whatever we know of friendship and goodness... whatever we know of joy and peace and beauty — that has put us in touch with God.

If we delight in wind, sun, rain, the ocean... if we delight in the human body... if we cherish ourselves and others, thrill with our beloved, play with our children — then we can be praising God. If we are celebrating at a party, God is there. Because

God's "delight" is to be with the children of men and women, there is no celebration, no reason to praise, without him. The Psalmist advises, "If you delight in the Lord, he will give you your heart's desire" (Ps 37:4). And what do we desire in our heart of hearts but unending love, peace, joy?

Where love is, there is God. We have come together to celebrate truth, beauty, goodness, in all their forms and in their ultimate form in the world.

With a hymn of praise directed for the most part to the Lord Jesus Christ, we recognize God's intimate presence in each of us, and in all of us together. But, most of all, we acknowledge God's greatness, glory, and mercy in himself.

For those of us who have been immersed from childhood on in the Church's liturgical seasons, perhaps there is no better way of seeing God's goodness — and our own goodness as a result — than to meditate on the Scriptures. "With the Holy Spirit, in the glory of God the Father" and with Jesus, our Lord, the real source of our repentance, and consequent forgiveness, let us listen to the conclusion of Psalm 51. Hear the deep emotions the repentant sinner experiences as he praises God:

Let me hear the sounds of joy and gladness;
    the bones you have crushed shall rejoice....
Give me back the joy of your salvation,
    and a willing spirit sustain in me....
O Lord, open my lips,
    and my mouth shall proclaim your praise.
For you are not pleased with sacrifices;
    should I offer a holocaust, you would not accept it.
My sacrifice, O God, is a contrite spirit;
    a heart contrite and humbled, O God, you will not spurn.
                                        (Ps 51:9, 10, 12-19)

PRAYER

Lord, thank you for your life in me. Thank you for the good in my life, for Jesus through "whom all good things come." Thank you for enlightening my mind and kindling my heart to understand your great goodness and mercy!

II

The Way of Illuminative Reformation

THE FOLLOWING OF CHRIST

"Come to me all you who labor and are burdened,
and I will give you rest. Take my yoke upon your shoulders and
learn from me for I am gentle and humble of heart.
Your souls will find rest,
for my yoke is easy and my burden light."
(Mt 11:26-30)

THE LITURGY OF THE WORD

"Lord, you have the words of everlasting life."

13. The Readings

Here, if we listen, our enlightenment continues on the way of reforming our lives according to the pattern and the light manifested to us in Jesus and confirmed by the Holy Spirit. On the mountain of the transfiguration, a voice from the cloud said, "This is my beloved Son, with whom I am well pleased; listen to him" (Mt 17:5).

Holy Scripture shows us that from the time when human beings, Adam and Eve, walked and talked with God in the garden, we have treasured God's presence. Pilgrims of the Absolute, we falter without a secure hold, without direction.

Our Jewish ancestors, the people of God of old, had the ark of the covenant and the tablets of the law which they carried to remind them that their God, their rock, defender and guide, was near.

We have Jesus, our exemplar, guide, and Savior. We have the Scriptures and the Eucharist. Our God is near, especially at Mass.

But the Scriptures (and what we do at Mass) are more complex than at first we understand. God speaks to us… but the sacred writings contain more than the words that are preceded by "God said."

The Scriptures are a record of what God *did*, of what God did among his people, and what God *is doing* among us. They are a record of God's life among his human creation. God has spoken not only in words, but in people, in events, in the saving history in which we are all involved. We can experience this at Mass.

27

One of the great anxieties of our time is so many people's feeling of rootlessness. No one cares, we think in times of despair, not even God... if, indeed, God is not "dead." We may have a home, a place to be ourselves, a family in which to find ourselves, and friends... yet the feeling persists.

The reason for our restlessness — a blessed restlessness, if we only knew — is that we have roots deeper than our immediate forebears. We have been around longer than our chronological age would imply, and we will remain beyond our fleeting years. We have a past and a future, a family history, a link with all humanity, past, present, and future.

Abraham and Sarah, Moses, Matthew, Mark, Luke, and John... Mary, Peter, and Paul, and especially Jesus, tell us that family history: "At various times in the past and in various ways, God spoke to our ancestors through the prophets; but in our own time, the last days, he has spoken to us through his Son" (Heb 1:1-2).

PRAYER

Lord, I am always desiring that you speak to me. But you do speak to me in many ways, and in many disguises. It is not that you do not speak. It is I who do not listen. Open my ears and my heart, Lord, to hear you especially in your holy word.

14. The Bible: God's Guidance for Our Formation

The Bible is the perennial bestseller. Of course, it is good literature, has famous authors, is a good story with wide human interest and popular appeal, significant social contribution, full of meaning, historically important, an exciting achievement, a landmark. Even with all that, it is found on many coffee tables, but not in as many minds and hearts.

But why should it really be the "bestseller" of all time? It is God's book, the word of God, the revelation of God to us. From it we learn our beginnings, we learn of the God who first loved us. We learn of Jesus, the Son of God. In it we find the explanation of our existence, our human and divine meaning. The Bible is our story, our family history. It shows forth the humanity of God in God's dealings and relationships with us, God's interventions in history.

God is our God, and we are his people. God's word is power and light and sweetness. All this is everlastingly good news, but only so if we listen to God's word and carry out its directions for our lives.

PRAYER

The hearts of the disciples on the way to Emmaus "burned within them" when you opened the Scriptures to them, Lord. Why does not my heart burn within me as it did with the disciples on the way to Emmaus with the resurrected Lord when I hear your word in the readings and the homily at Mass? Help me to understand the great gift of your word.

15. Our Spiritual "Formation Field"

The Scriptures, as we noted, are our story, our family history. They are also an outline of the areas of our lives in which we are formed and work out our salvation, our spiritual "formation field."[5]

The Scriptures, old and new, point out to us our spiritual forebears, our spiritual heritage; they are the story of our ances-

---

[5] Cf. van Kaam and Muto, *Becoming Spiritually Mature.*

tors in the faith. They point us to Jesus and his life and work, the pattern for our inspiration and our imitation.

Let's continue to look at how spiritual formation happens. As noted, we are continually being "formed," and we are continually forming and influencing others in our homes, our workplace, our world. Formation spirituality identifies four spheres of life experience as our spiritual "formation field" with, most especially, God at the center (cf. graph below[6]). These spheres of people, events and things contain "directives" that influence and shape our spiritual unfolding and growth in formative and, unfortunately, sometimes in deformative, ways.

Mediated, Cosmic, and World Formation
(Social Responsibilities)

Inner Formation of	Holy Trinity	Inter-Relational
Our Heart	Father, Son, Spirit	Formation in
(Wholistic Spirituality)	God, the Divine Forming	Community
	Mystery	(Relationships)
	Immediate	
	Situational Formation	
	(Formation Atmosphere)	

God, Our Center

First, at the center of our formation field is God the Father, Jesus, the Holy Spirit — the Divine Forming Mystery. There is no spiritual formation that does not have God as its center.

God is the Source, and we need to know our Source if we are to know how to return to that Source. The Scriptures show

---

6 Cf. Muto and van Kaam, Workbook, p. 5, Course Two, "Growing in Christ Through Our Relationships," a six-part course in Spiritual Formation for People in Ministry, Epiphany Association, 1998.

us how to follow the way back to God in terms of our inner life, our relationships, our immediate situation, and our wider world.

Jesus on the Cross, with blood and water gushing from his pierced side, demonstrates to us how, through Baptism (water) and the Eucharist (blood), we are sent on this spiritual journey back to the Father with the help of his Holy Spirit (fire).

As preparation for our journey, we would do well to listen to our ancestors and forebears in the faith. Our first readings at every Mass tell us their story, and most of all about what they discovered our God is like.

Here we learn that we have been "*pre-formed*" in love, in God's image and likeness, and that we are always becoming the unique original "I" that God, in loving kindness and goodness, created us to be. We are always "on the way" of faithful formation, reformation and, in hope, graced transformation.

We are told this wondrous story and history in the inspired Old Testament, particularly in the Psalms, which set the tone and voice the sentiments of the prayer we express in response to God's word. (The Psalter, says the *Catechism of the Catholic Church*, is the book in which the word of God becomes man's prayer. It is the prayer of the People of God, which prophesies our salvation and looks forward to its fulfillment.) Our salvation history continues to be sketched out for us in the Church's meditation on Jesus' words and actions in the New Testament, in the Gospels and the Acts of the Apostles, and the Epistles of St. Paul.

Inner Life

The first quadrant of our formation field is our inner life, the spiritual formation of our hearts in the dispositions and disciplines of the "children of God." Unlike the ideas we might have about the spiritual life — something that monks and nuns "have"

— our spiritual journey involves all of our living, our entire hearts — our "core form" — the center of our sensing, feeling, thinking, willing, decision making, all of our rich and complex inner life.

Thus the "spiritual life" is more than our prayer life, or our going to Mass. It involves all of our thoughts, words, and actions, our entire human and spiritual participation in life. It is intimately intertwined with our relationships, our situations, all that we influence and all that influences us.

Here we recognize that we are influenced spiritually, for better or worse, in many ways, especially by our own hearts in how we think and feel about things, people, and events. The Scriptures, the Readings of the liturgy of the Mass, help to inform and form all of our living, in the so-called "evangelical virtues": about things (the spirit of poverty), about events (the spirit of obedience), and about people (chaste, unselfish love). They do this in the way of the imitation of Christ through reflection and prayer and meditation on the life and teachings of Jesus.

Relationships

The second area of our spiritual formation field is that of our relationships, our "interformational formation in community" (*inter*, from the Latin, meaning between).

Think about the relationships from the time you were born — your sociohistorical background, your parents, brothers and sisters, relatives, friends, teachers, priests, nuns, business associates, co-workers, professional people, and on and on. We are formed by them; they are formed by us. These influences go on throughout our lifetime.

In all these relationships, we are in our own unique way to be Jesus. How do I do so if I am not striving to know, love, and serve him in myself and others, if I do not listen in faith and in obedient submission to his directives for my relationships in the Scriptures I hear at Mass or my own meditation on them?

Situations

The third sphere of spiritual influence is that of our immediate situations in life, the places, things, and events in our immediate environment that directly affect our thought and action, and upon which we also have an impact: the school we attend, the church where we worship, our home, our work situations.

We are "not an island." God did not intend that we be saved alone. We are on our spiritual journey in the community of our relationships in family and friends. We are also dwellers in the "community" of our environments, in our immediate society, and in the wider world.

Wider World

The fourth area of our formation field encompasses the wider world, its influence, for example, through the media, for good or bad, on our spiritual formation, internal and external. It affects our attitudes toward the environment, toward war and peace, toward social justice, toward poverty and the oppressed of the world.

We, in our prosperous United States, do not live in a vacuum in our isolated communities, but amidst pockets of human destitution worldwide. Who is to administer God's care, if we do not?

PRAYER

Lord, deepen our perspective, inspire us to see our everyday living as never before. Help us to appreciate that we are an entire field of formation with you as our source and center. Guide us in bringing all the facets of our lives into the light and love of your presence.

16. Re-formation Through the Imitation of Christ

Ordinarily when people think of the imitation of Christ, they have in mind the medieval spiritual classic of Thomas à Kempis, *The Imitation of Christ*. That is a very fine book for reflection and prayer, but it is not what we are speaking about here.

First of all, God's call to us is at once simple and complex. Jesus said simply, "Follow me." Simple, because Jesus is simple; complex, because we are complicated creatures, all involved in mystery. God calls us to be "perfect as your heavenly Father is perfect." That's clear enough.

The problem is, we do not even know what perfection is, and more important, we can't reach "perfection" on our own. Another translation of the ending to Jesus' famed Sermon on the Mount, as we noted above, has it that we are *"to be made* perfect." But that is still a complex make-over job!

Jesus, of course, is the model for our imitation. But he is also the enabler of that formation by the grace of his life, death, and resurrection freely given. He did give us a road map: Obey the commandments of the Old Covenant to love God above all things, with all your heart, mind, and strength, and your neighbor as yourself. In the beatitudes of the New Covenant, Jesus lays out an impossible (if we try to do it alone) way to follow him: "Blessed are the poor, the humble, the persecuted...." Love me, as "I have loved you," he tells us, is the way of living and laying down our lives.

We cannot do that alone; thank God, we are not alone. Jesus is with us every step of the way.

PRAYER

Yes, Lord, we do thank you that we are not alone. Along with Jesus we have our family, our friends, our co-workers, all the people of God. We are pilgrims on a journey and Jesus is the way, the truth, and the life.

17. Three Ways of Following

1. The first way of following Jesus is the way of exterior *"behavioral imitation."*[7] This way of following is a necessary beginning, but it has its shortcomings. For example, the following of Christ suggested in the contemporary question, "What would Jesus do?", might be merely focusing on the external pattern of the Jesus of the gospels as he lived in his time, and comparing it to my own actions.

This way does not neglect Jesus' inner attitudes, but notices mainly the words and actions of Jesus that reveal how he lived them. It may point to inner transformation, but there is the ever human problem of stopping at external behavior in action and appearance. Note, however, in line with our theme, the goal is "purifying formation" of our intention and our motives.

2. The second way of following Jesus is the way of *"intimate imitation."* It draws my attention to the inner life of Jesus. I strive for the dispositions of the heart, the same feelings and attitudes that I see in him. These dispositions become "habits of the heart" that inform all my relationships. Here are the echoes of "illuminating reformation," getting our ego selves out of the way.

In this way I aspire to imitate the inner life of Christ as seen

---

[7] The following material is taken from Adrian van Kaam's *On Being Yourself*, pp. 182-191, as presented in the Epiphany Association's ELFA (Epiphany Lay Formation Academy) '99 Workbook, pp. 80-82.

in the Scriptures, forming my intellectual and vital emotional being in the way of intimacy with God. This is a great grace "to be accepted with gratitude," according to van Kaam, and perhaps this is my call for a lifetime. Many people are called to this kind of following and imitation of Christ.

3. In the third way of imitation, God gives an extraordinary grace — the way of the saints, of "transforming identification." Here "I am not only present to Christ; Christ also becomes inwardly present to me in an undeniably mysterious manner." According to our theme, the ultimate purpose of the Eucharist is "unifying transformation."

However we are called, uniquely and in community, we are called to follow Christ. In the Mass we ask for the courage and the grace to choose this way. "God cannot inspire unrealizable desires," says St. Thérèse of Lisieux. In the Epistle to the Philippians, St. Paul advises us from whence our great desires come: "Work with anxious concern to achieve your salvation. It is God who in his good will toward you, begets in you any measure of desire or achievement" (vs. 12-14a). St. Paul describes our ultimate following and fulfillment:

> God has given us the wisdom to understand fully the mystery, the plan he was pleased to decree in Christ, to be carried out in the fullness of time: namely, to bring all things in the heavens and on earth into one under Christ's leadership (Eph 1:9-10).

That is our unique and communal destiny. Do we not detect in Scripture the assumption that God has a greater stake in our spiritual health and in our salvation than we do ourselves? After all, the Father sent his Son Jesus to us to make it possible. If Jesus' life, ministry, death, and resurrection does not accomplish God's purposes, that indeed would be tragic.

PRAYER

Jesus, model and ever-present Savior, lead us and guide us through our reflection and prayer in the Mass to our everlasting destiny with you. Let us understand that our efforts alone in our pride, or complacency in our sloth, are insults to your gracious mercy and love. Form, reform, and transform us in your image and likeness.

18. Preaching the Word

First of all, the word of God in Scripture is crucial for our spiritual formation. This is expressed vividly by the prophet Isaiah: "My word that goes forth does not come back to me without accomplishing that for which I sent it" (55:11).

The word is power. There can be little doubt of this in a time when a word can cause a revolution. The people will move toward "peace" or "justice for all" or "clean environment" when the time is right, when the word expresses an idea whose time has come.

The inspired word of God is power, too. God said, "Let there be light," and light was made. When we hear the word of God something happens in us... if our hearts are right. And because we hear the word, something will happen in the world too, in God's good time.

The readings at Mass, the Church teaches, are the "word of God." The word of God "in the words of man," Scripture scholars add. These words are powerful if we will listen.

But to be heard effectively today, the word of God needs to be translated into terms we can understand in our own situation in our daily lives. It has to be translated into what God wants to say to us *here and now*. It is God's word, but God speaks in our own language.

Some preachers, including ourselves, may *use* the word rather than proclaim it. But God's word, like God himself, will not be "used" to push anyone's pride, to back anyone's prejudice, to push anyone's politics. God's word is "a two-edged sword." It cuts to the heart and to the marrow; it judges all thoughts. Today, more than ever, we need the word that reconciles rather than the rhetoric that separates.

"You have heard it said... but I say to you, love your enemies, do good to those who hate you and say all manner of things against you."

How do we know when it is God who speaks?

We can be sure that God is speaking — in anyone's language, and in the humblest attempt to communicate — if it results in an effective call to love, to witness, to openness, to service, to truth, to humility, to understanding, to a passion for justice, to the wisdom of creative suffering... to the will to reach ever more deeply into life and persons and God so that "all things may be restored in Christ."

PRAYER

Lord, so often in your parables you cautioned the people on how they were to listen. You said, "You who have ears to hear, let them hear!" Sometimes my heart is not open, so I hear only what I want to hear. Other times I need discernment to hear your word amidst many human words. Lord, open my heart... and my understanding.

19. Listening to the Word

We may expect both too much and too little from the preacher stepping forward to give the homily. We may expect too much when we expect that person to entertain us with a story and some rhetoric, to transform himself into something he is not, or to give back to us only our own prejudices in interpreting the Scriptures.

We expect too little when we don't expect the preacher to be prepared. It is the homilist's business to know more than we do about the time, place, and peculiar circumstances of the original setting of the readings. We expect too little as well when we don't expect the homilist to translate the message into present terms, to clarify concretely the meaning and how it applies to us right now.

Still, for our part, we have to listen, really listen, not just to the preacher and the always too meager words, but to the Spirit who is always active wherever the word of God is being spoken and being talked about. No matter what else may be wrong, the Spirit is present among us gathered together, and the Spirit is ready to in-spirit us with the truth of life if we are listening.

But what does it mean to listen, to really listen? The word for listen is related to obedience, from the Latin verb *ob audire,* which means *to listen attentively to.* Obedience is absolutely necessary for any following of Christ.

Scripture repeats over and over the necessity of obedience, a lasting disposition of the heart, that "disposes" us to the readiness to follow the directives of God for our lives from wherever and from whomever they come. St. Paul urges us to "be obedient, as servants of Christ, doing the will of God from the heart" (Eph 6:5-6).

PRAYER

Lord, do I really expect to hear you speak during the homily at Mass? Have I allowed my hearing — and my expectation — to grow dull? Forgive me, Lord, for not trusting you to speak to me in a way you have designed for me. I need to hear your word.

20. How Do We Listen?

We listen with our entire self.

As noted, "God ultimately intends for us to live lives that are whole, complete, and at peace. This happiness can be ours only if we follow the lead of grace and begin to 'sound together' in harmony with the Divine Forming Mystery at the center of our formation field."[8] "Sounding together," is described by St. Augustine as *harmonica partium consonantia,* or the harmonious sounding together of the parts.

When we are on the way toward the way of our formation in Christ, when we are listening to his word and acting on it, we begin to be in harmony with God's "consonant" (harmonious) design for our lives. Hence, the beginning of lives of peace and joy.

Father van Kaam describes a method of appraising our progress in living harmonious lives by taking note of what formation spirituality calls the "C's of Consonance." This is the "transcendent" way, one that focuses on the aspirations and inspirations that come from our human spirit rather than the impulses and ambitions that stem only from our pre-transcendent natures, namely, our isolated socio-historical, vital, and functional dimensions. It is a way of following Christ in our everyday lives.

---

[8] Van Kaam and Muto, *Becoming Spiritually Mature,* Formation Guide, p. 79. See the Video Series for an elaboration of this and the following material.

In my spirit I know that I yearn for something more than what I may experience in my everyday, ordinary life. I long to be in harmony with my sometimes "difficult" relationships, work situation, and world. Why do I feel fragmented and confused? Is it because some of my desires, thoughts, and actions are not in tune with my call? Do I lose my vision of God as my center? What deformative dispositions, such as being in control of self and others, or excessive worry about myself or others, or anxiety about the future, do I need to change? Do I really believe that God intends for me to live a life that is whole, complete, and at peace?

The C's of Consonance (harmony) can point out a way of appraising my spiritual health:

Congeniality: This disposition is most foundational. To be congenial is to be at home with my "genesis," with what God has created me to be from my birth. In my heart, am I always being true to myself and to others, to my situations in life, and with God's call in all this?

Compatibility: To be compatible is to be and to feel comfortable, to be able to work with others in the relationships in my situations in life: family, work, church, society. It is to be firm but flexible in all my relationships.

Compassionate: To be compassionate is to realize that neither I nor anyone else is perfect, that we are all deformed in some way. We need to be able to be kind and gentle with ourselves, to be able to "suffer with" others, to empathize with them in their life situations.

When we are congenial, compatible, and compassionate, then we can be:

Competent: To be competent is develop and use all my abilities and talents in aspiring to be what God intends for me to be. More than being "efficient," it involves higher motives and aspirations.

But, you object, these are impossible ideals in my condition and situations!

God is aware of your problems and your deepest needs. God knows where you are coming from. God knows our human heritage. As we noted above, we have a family history that affects us for good or bad.

Formation spirituality points out four dimensions of our being: the sociohistorical (our family background), the vital (our body and its needs), the functional (our productive life), and the transcendent (our spirit). In every area of our "formation field," these human dimensions play a role. We are, in a sense, our "formation field" in each of these spheres: our inner life, our relationships, our situations, our world. As noted, we are formed in each of these areas of our lives; we influence them, they influence us.

Modern psychology has taught us to probe into our psyches, in our "socio-historical" dark and light sides. God knows this history better than we do, and he aids us in our search if we let him. Our "vital dimension," our personal bodily natures, are sometimes a mystery to us, but not to our Creator. And, today, we know the pull and the force that our "functional" demands place upon us by our society, whose only goal, it seems at times, is production and achievement at any human cost. We are not as familiar with our "transcendent dimension," the spiritual aspirations and inspirations that come to us and should pervade our entire beings, socio-historical, vital, and functional.

PRAYER

Lord, help me to listen attentively, and to follow your call in all of my being and activity. Let your guidance and inspiration flow through me in harmony with my family, my relationships, my situations, my life in your world. Your word is a living word. Help me to live your word in my life.

THE PROFESSION OF FAITH

21. The Creed: Someone to Believe In

There was a time when we studied the Creed mostly as a catalogue of "truths" to be believed. Now we understand that it is also the revealing history of Someone to *believe in.*

You can believe the truth that God is Father, but unless you ponder all that he has done for you as his prime creation (or if you have not experienced true "fathering" in your life), you may not be able to experience God as Father deserving of your confidence. It may be a problem of our image of God.

Indeed, God created the world, as he ordered all things in it under our human dominion. But what good, if we do not at times, at least, consciously touch God's ever-active and sustaining presence?

Truthfully, God in Jesus became one of us and suffered and died "for our sake," but how weak is our faith until we begin to trace God's redeeming features in the universe the Creator has made, in your own spirit, and in the people God loves?

With faith you can believe that the Spirit is here animating this community gathering and confirming us in our love and service of one another. It evokes a response of openness of mind and heart.

We have been born into God's family through creation, initiated into this Christian community through Baptism, nourished and sustained in the risen Christ through the ordained and lay ministry and our care for each other. But we will not really experience this holy relationship until we begin to live this truth in our homes and in our workplaces.

PRAYER

Lord, to believe in you, is to trust that what you have created me to be will come to be in me if I am faithful. The Creed tells me that you are on my side. It is the love story of your relationship with your people. Sharpen my awareness of your everloving and merciful care.

22. A Mighty Creed

"We believe in One God, the Father the Almighty."

Our creed is a mighty creed about a mighty God. It is incredible, unbelievable! And that is what makes it a profession of faith.

"We believe in One God, the Father the Almighty..." not maker of bridges, or builder of skyscrapers, or stacker of fortunes, or molder of civilizations; not king, dictator, astronaut... but, "maker of heaven and earth."

But an almighty Father might seem to many to be intimidating, particularly if we have not, as noted, experienced strong, yet tender, fathering when we were young. Some people never get over the experience of a "bad childhood."

God is not like our human fathers. The *Catechism of the Catholic Church* advises that we "cleanse our hearts of certain images drawn 'from this world'" [2779]. Those indeed may be coming from our own distorted personal or cultural conditioning. It may be well to examine our image of God: do we think of God as a stern taskmaster and administer of punishment or as a loving parent, solicitous for our human and spiritual health? No image as such is adequate to contain the mystery of "Our Father who art in heaven."

Listen to the Letter to the Romans on the kind of God we have:

> If God is for us, who can be against us? Is it possible that he who did not spare his own Son but handed him over for the sake of us all will not grant us all things besides? Who shall bring a charge against God's chosen ones? God, who justifies? Who shall condemn them? Christ Jesus, who died or rather was raised up, who is at the right hand of God and who intercedes for us? (Rm 8: 31-34).

"We believe in Jesus Christ"

We believe "in Jesus Christ, his only Son… born of a virgin," who died for us, "And on the third day rose from the dead." Again, an incredible, "unbelievable" confession of faith. This same Jesus is the everlasting Son of God, who was and who is with the Father from all eternity, but who has become one of us in the flesh, in time, being "like us in all things except sin." It is he who is our help and our salvation. If we have any tendency to doubt that, listen again to the Letter to the Romans:

> Who will separate us from the love of Christ? Trial, or distress, or persecution, or hunger, or nakedness, or danger, or the sword? As Scripture says, "For your sake we are being slain all the day long; we are looked upon as sheep to be slaughtered." Yet in all this we are more than conquerors because of him who has loved us. For I am certain that neither death nor life, neither the present nor the future, neither angels nor principalities, neither the present nor the future, nor powers, neither height nor depth nor any creature, will be able to separate us from the love of God that comes to us in Christ Jesus, our Lord (Rm 8:35-39).

"We believe in the Holy Spirit the Lord and giver of life"

The Holy Spirit is the breath and nourisher of life in us. Jesus lives within us through his Spirit. How incredibly wonderful! We believe "in the resurrection of the dead and life everlasting." We not only can, but do believe that, because God himself has taught us in Jesus to reach for the stars — believing the unbelievable, dreaming the impossible, living forever because God is God.

PRAYER

Lord, you teach me to expect great things. Yet, my life is made up of mostly rather dull, routine, everyday things. But that really is not so, if I read your mighty creed rightly. Your everlasting life is even now enlivening every deed I do, every step I take with the Father's loving, constant care, with Jesus as savior and model, and with the Holy Spirit's nourishing breath, strength and guidance.

23. Faith: What It Means to Believe

Faith, according to St. Paul, is "…the evidence of things not seen and the hope of things to come." That is a definition for the mind. Faith also means to live by faith, or to be *faithful*. That is a definition for the heart. It means a willing obedience to the way in which God is directing our lives.

It may help to understand this disposition of the heart, one which is absolutely necessary for our spiritual growth, by attempting to describe how we come to faith. Faith, says St. Paul again, "comes through hearing." Most of us have learned of faith at our mother's knee. For many old-timers, faith, as we heard it, was accompanied by fear of an awesome God who was also a judging and punishing God.

This kind of faith can be perhaps the beginning of what Scripture calls the fear of the Lord, that is "the beginning of wisdom." Unfortunately, because of others' rigor or our own, fear of God often turned into a servile, fearful submission motivated primarily by fear of punishment.

If we are fortunate, we may have come to understand the fear of God in a more benign way as reverence or "awe," as described by Father van Kaam:

> Awe is dread become reverence under the transformation of a loving abandonment to the Mystery that draws us by its beneficence while at the same time keeping us at a humble distance by its majesty.[9]

Everyone, according to van Kaam, is born with a predisposition for *awe*. In other words, awe is the human person's foundational religious experience, that of being substantially united with the Divine. But awe, like faith, is above sense perception; it is transcendent, it speaks of the "more than," that is, more than the socio-historical, the vital, and the functional dimensions of our human persons.

Taking our minds and hearts deeper into our selves, awe "disposes us to a life of enlightened presence to the mystery of people, events, and things in their deepest being."[10] It allows us, in other words, to see into the deepest purpose of all that God created. Even in the darkness of the faith, awe "makes us present to the Mystery," no matter what is going on in our lives.

Awe also disposes us to what theologians call the "theo-

---

[9] Van Kaam, *Human Formation*, Formation Spirituality, Volume II, p. 213.
[10] Muto and van Kaam, ECP Workbook, p. 71.

logical virtues" of faith, hope, and love. "It is the secret source of our consonance, our peace of heart, mind, and body; it is the spring of faith, hope, and love, of firmness and courage in the midst of adversity."[11]

A good example of how this disposition of awe filters down through our being into the virtues of faith, hope, and love can be shown in parents with a child. A child's spirituality is awakened by the loving sounds and motion that surrounds the infant; this is the child's initial identification with the God-given spirit of the parents and is the beginning of the child's assimilation of the dispositions that will serve its growth throughout life. Awe about the wonder of beauty, truth, and love makes life worth living. If we do not somehow grasp how "awe-filled and wonderfully made" we are (cf. Psalm 139), we remain woefully unaware of our awesome potential. So much more is this true for our children. If left unattended in a child, it becomes what is known as "formation ignorance,"[12] a disease of the soul that some people never overcome. Wittingly or unwittingly, parents become the channels through which this grace of "living water" flows or the blockages that impede the flow.

The child, even from the womb, receives this gift of faith, hope, and love through its parents. Parents transfer this gift in their loving care for infants and children, in touching, speaking, and feeding them. Watch the attentive and loving mother caress her child, speak to it in loving sounds, care for its bodily needs. From this the child, even as a newborn infant, learns that someone has faith in them, trusts them, has great hopes for them, and loves them unconditionally, just for themselves alone. That is what our faith tells us God does for us!

---

[11] Ibid., p. 193.

[12] Van Kaam, *Transcendent Formation, Formation Spirituality*, Volume VI, p. 46.

From this initial firm foundation, the child appreciates who they are, and when older, who others are as God's loved creation, and can reciprocate in awe, faith, hope, and love.

PRAYER

Lord, please teach me how to appreciate how crucial faith is in my life and in the life of others in my care. Let me be a channel of your faith, hope, and love, experiencing at the same time your love for me. Let me always be in awe of your loving presence in my life and the life of others.

24. Opening Our Hearts: Essential for Following Christ

To review: the heart is the center of our affections and our willing. It is the deepest part of us, where our thinking, feeling, willing, imagining, and anticipating come together and help us make decisions about living and loving. It is our "core form," the sensible and responsible ground of our affective life through which everyday life is filtered, and which through its dispositions shapes us, our character and personality.[13] This process of going from the mind to the heart may be likened to the homely action of a "marination" process in which the "meat" of firm instruction becomes palatable and digestible.

Many of us often live on the surface of life. Perhaps we do not live from our core or heart, the seat of Christlike love and life in the center of our being. We are often at a loss to know our true self, the self that has been formed by God in the image of Jesus Christ. We are not always able to identify the source of our desires, thoughts, and actions. Do these spring from family back-

---

[13] Van Kaam, op. cit., p. 166.

ground (socio-historical dimension), bodily needs (vital dimension), work (functional dimension), or spirit (transcendent dimension)?

In our society today, we do not easily identify the "dynamic strivings" that move us. What gets us going: movements, trends or fads (sociological pulsations), impulses or addictions (vital pulsations), the need to succeed (functional ambition), or my heart (transcendent inspirations and aspirations)?

One or another of our dispositions can dominate our life, can channel all our energy and account for our actions. The human being can live mostly for pleasure (vital), satisfaction (functional), or joy (transcendent). According to the great Commandment, all thoughts, words and actions for the Christian ought to be oriented toward ultimate meaning and purpose. For that to happen, of course, our spiritual formation is possible only through the grace of God. We must be humble and submissive enough to admit that we can't do it by ourselves.

Opening our hearts to the transcendent is the primary disposition that lets us hear the voice of God for the following of Christ in our life. Openness to, and reliance upon the saving power of God is a gift. With that gift, in awe we sense that we are invited to an intimate relationship with the Trinity in co-forming and co-creating life, world, and universe.

PRAYER

Lord, let me begin to see that all of life is gift, everything — people, places, events — is grace. Open my heart to receive the gifts you so generously impart. In gratitude help me to share these gifts in all areas of my life.

GENERAL INTERCESSIONS:
PRAYER OF THE FAITHFUL

25. In Imitation of Christ

What is uppermost in your thoughts when you get yourself together before the Lord? Family or personal troubles or hopes? A sick relative? Your own inarticulate longings for the simple presence of God, for a personal understanding of God's word, for knowledge of God's will in your life and for the capacity to hear and obey? Your list is probably quite standard.

The question is, is our prayer a prayer of faith, or is it merely a litany of needs, asking God for favors? Do we pray with confidence, or do we utter only a self-centered cry?

Recently, prayer of petition has fallen into some disfavor. It is said that our prayer should be more than "gimme," and of course it should. But an authority above all spiritual masters tells us: "Ask, and you shall receive." A wise person has said that all prayer, even that of adoration, reparation, and thanksgiving, is really basically prayer of petition. In every prayer, particularly the asking one, we recognize God's love and mercy, we express our confidence in the One who can do something to help us. Which is really to let God be God.

But there is more behind the feeling about petitionary prayer. The danger is to think that once we have prayed, our task is finished. We sit back and wait for something to happen.

If we can do something about our situation, obviously we must. And, if we examine ourselves truthfully, we know that we can do *something* about most any problem, at least we can change our attitude toward it. Sometimes we are called on only to stand firm and not to fear. To pray with faith is to be *faithful*.

Do we pray for peace in the family? In the world? Begin

also to work for it. Prayer doesn't change God. Prayer changes us. If we really pray, God will give us the heart to change, or to bear with patience what we cannot change.

PRAYER

"God, grant me the serenity to accept the things I cannot change; the courage to change the things I can; and the wisdom to know the difference" (Reinhold Niebuhr).

26. A Scriptural Reflection on Prayer

St. James puts prayer in a tough, but instructive, context — the struggle and pain of trial in life, the common experience of pray-ers:

Count it pure joy when you are involved in every kind of trial. Realize that when your faith is tested this makes for endurance. Let endurance come to its perfection so that you may be fully mature and lacking in nothing (Jm 1:2-4).

St. James continues to set up the atmosphere for prayer, the sentiments and dispositions of the heart that reach the heart of Christ:

If any of you is without wisdom, let him ask it from God who gives generously and ungrudgingly to all, and it will be given him. But he must ask in faith, never doubting, for the doubter is like the surf tossed and driven by the wind. The person of this sort, devious and erratic in all that he does, must not expect to receive anything from the Lord (Jm 1:5-7).

Because of the Church, that is all Christians, we do not come to Mass to pray only for ourselves. The prayer of the Church at Mass is "public," not private prayer. We do pray for ourselves, but in the intercessions, we pray first cf all for the needs of the Church and the world: The Holy Father and the ministers of the Church and for the leaders of our country and world. We pray for wisdom, and with faith.

We Pray for Ourselves, for All People

The time has come for the people to pray for the people of God. Unabashedly, we now pray a prayer of petition.

— That all may be well with the "important" people of the Church.... That all may be well with the leaders of the state... for together these are as big as life, affecting all our lives.

— They exist for us humans, inevitably religious and social, who forever need the initiative, organization, and leadership that, under the Holy Spirit, makes community possible — people working and living together, brothers and sisters all.

— That all people everywhere: black, white, yellow, brown, red... rich, poor, middle class... overfed and starving... naked and multi-wardrobed — that each be blessed according to each person's peculiar need.

— That our city, our town, our parish community... that this assembly of people who have come together... that our friends, brothers and sisters, parents, living and dead, may all be well.

And me, too, Lord, give me what I need.

III

The Way of Unifying Transformation

THE LITURGY OF THE EUCHARIST:
UNION AND COMMUNION

"Anyone who loves me will be true to my word,
and my Father will love them; we will come to them
and make our home in them."
(Jn 14:23)

27. Preparation of the Gifts

"Blessed are you, Lord, God of all creation. Through your goodness we have this bread and wine to offer."

A family, or a representative grouping of different elements in the parish family, brings up the bread and wine. People of all types and classes offer gifts. What better symbolic action than God's people moving forward to the altar, their hands bearing fruits of their common existence.

Bread and wine represent us... our work, our lives, all that we are and all that we have. People in some parishes bring up gifts for the poor.

Having the collection offering brought up at this time is a significant gesture. It is a way of calling attention to an important fact in modern life: that our wealth too represents us, our labor, our sacrifices, our human efforts, our very selves.

Is our concern the family? The poor? Equal housing? Equal opportunity in hiring? Education? Family assistance? Peace? It's all going to take money... our own and other people's. We may have to tighten our belts, to live more simply, to give, so that others might simply live.

We all contribute something as we offer our gifts now, so that all can participate with dignity at the banquet table.

PRAYER

Lord, I bring the "bread" of my body, my mind, my strength, my work, my family, my church. I bring the "wine" of my emotions, my sweat, my tears, my heart's desire. I give them to you. Jesus make of them an offering worthy of God's gifts to me.

28. Bread and Wine

In coming to Mass, we have come to a celebration different from any other celebration. It is a highly ritualized celebration because only by means of sign and symbol can all the richness of its reality be even obscurely expressed.

We are celebrating Christ, great mystery and great sacrament, in the way he asked us to. We are celebrating Christ with a sacrificial meal, not with a big meal with much to eat and drink, but a meal like the Last Supper, where there was a coming together of Christ's friends, communication, and love — above all, the love of the One who was going to die for the others.

Along with Christ, we are celebrating all those who together with Christ died yesterday and will live and die today and tomorrow — like him, for others. We enter into this celebration completely only if we can count ourselves among the Christs of tomorrow.

The sign of this celebration of love, of life-death-resurrection love, is bread and wine — classical symbols of food and drink, of nourishment and exhilaration, of life from death, of body and blood.

We the people bring up bread and wine now, signs of ourselves to be made into a sign of Christ.

PRAYER

Lord, what kind of sign does my life-offering project? Is the gift I make of myself only a gesture without meaning, or can people see some of your gift to them in my gift? Does the giving of my gift at Mass open me to sacrificial giving in my everyday life? May it be so, Lord, with your help.

29. Prayer Over the Gifts

Called by God, chosen from among the people, the priest stands for the people before the Lord.

The whole idea is archaic, some say. Ours is the day of the direct approach. We get what we want by going directly to the head person. No mediators need apply! We can dispense with priests, vestments, and ritual.

Furthermore, the argument goes, the gospel speaks first of poverty and active charity, of worshiping "in spirit and in truth." Why this liturgy which speaks of gifts, obligations, sacrifice, and even richness? Why this waste of purely symbolic human effort?

The argument deceives.

We may rightly question the efficacy of ritual alone to nourish the life of today's Christian: there is no scene more devoid of true religion than the pious on Sunday turning into the impious on Monday... or even the parking lot on Sunday!

But it would be supreme presumption to attempt to raise ourselves above the human condition, to think that we can dispense with the need to use sign and symbol to express the mystery of our relationship with God.

From the beginning human beings have offered gifts to their God, to solicit God's help, to express their complete dependence. And between the human offerer and God were always the priest and the altar. Not as a block to, but as a facilitator of, communication. Not a barrier between, but a link with.

Listen again to Pope John Paul:

As the Second Vatican Council teaches, "the faithful join in the offering of the Eucharist by virtue of their royal priesthood," yet it is the ordained priest who, "acting in the person of Christ, brings about the Eucharistic Sacrifice and offers it to God in the name of all the people." (Encyclical *On the Eucharist...*, chapter 3.)

Jesus was the only one to stand before the Father without a mediator. He took upon himself the burden of facing the unfaceable.

Yes, we have in God a loving parent, our Abba Father, one who is loving kindness itself. But we need Jesus to reveal that God to us. It is he who takes the gifts we offer through our priest and presents them to the God of us all. It is he who shows us how graciously they are accepted.

PRAYER

Jesus is my mediator with you, Father. St. Paul says that in Jesus, you have closed the barrier between us, and made the two of us one. You accept my gift because, in Jesus, my gift becomes his gift given back to you for me, for whom he died. I remember that especially at Mass.

30. "Work of Human Hands"

The bread and wine which the people have brought are the work of human hands. Human hands have raised the wheat. Human hands have planted the grapes. Seeds have fulfilled their promises.

Producing bread from wheat is a labor of hands, and wine from grapes a yet longer labor. The wheat gets ground and the grapes get crushed in the process to make something new. The new is something made out of the good things of earth. It is already a mixture of what humans have given and God has given. Always God and humankind are mixed up together.

We take what humanity has made and we offer it. Sometimes we ourselves have made this very same bread and wine. Or we *might* have made it. It is a familiar process, and we are able to identify ourselves with it.

But we can also identify God with it. God made the first move, and the second. God created the earth-potential for wheat and grape; God created us makers in his image.

We ask now that Christ join himself to our offering. He is the Father's Son and the "Son of man." He is our big brother, our true image before God.

PRAYER

Lord, it sometimes seems to me that I do not have, or am not, a suitable gift for offering. My work, which is not all that important or exciting, is done to feed and educate my family, to keep body and soul together. Even as I say that, Lord, I know that it is more than that. I am often distracted in my work, when I should be *doing what I am doing* with all my attention, because in that work is found your faithful presence.

31. "Your Sacrifice and Mine"

Up to this point in the Mass ritual there has been little mention of "sacrifice." Here, priest and people together, as representatives of all humanity, offer gifts of sacrifice. It is the supreme act of religion.

In his encyclical *On the Eucharist...*, the late Holy Father underscores the mystery of the Mass as Christ's sacrifice:

The Lord Jesus on the night he was betrayed (1 Cor 11:23) instituted the Eucharistic Sacrifice of his body and his blood. The words of the Apostle Paul bring us back to the dramatic setting in which the Eucharist was born. The Eucharist is indelibly marked by the event of the Lord's passion and death, of which it is not only a reminder but the sacramental representation. It is the sacrifice of the Cross perpetuated down the ages. (Chapter 1)

For all its hallowed tradition, however, the notion of sacrifice can be misunderstood. The word conjures up images of occult rites and tribal blood offerings.

We offer sacrifice, yes, but not as the ancients of old. They offered their victims to appease an angry god, or to exercise some kind of hold on godly power. We have gone beyond the bloody sacrifices and burnt offerings of the old Jewish law.

Our sacrifice is Christ's sacrifice: his body and blood offered up to save us and offered as food: sacramental sacrifice, sacramental food. Our sacrifice is a sacrifice of worship, a "clean oblation," the sacrifice of the new covenant. Our offering is Christ, the true worshiper:

> Sacrifice and oblation you did not want, but a body you prepared for me: in holocausts and sin-offerings you had no pleasure. Then I said, "Behold, I come to do your will, O God" (Heb 10:5-6).

We come to Mass to offer Christ, along with ourselves: all that we are and have and will ever be. When we offer our gifts we affirm that God is good and great and full of loving kindness. We confirm that life, in spite of all, is good. Because of Christ, all life is sacred, fit for giving, supremely suitable for celebration. All has been graced with God's presence and power.

Not everything in life, obviously, is immediately ready for offering. Making the world holy does not happen without its participating in sacrifice. The incarnation at present is in process, as yet incomplete. It will come to its fullness only with much effort directed and sustained by the power of God in Christ. The process is a fumbling one, full of failure. Our contribution entails the cross, suffering and setback. But with Paul we can say: We "fill up what is lacking in the sufferings of Christ."

PRAYER

Lord, you teach me that sacrifice is not necessarily something that I *give up*, but something I *take up* — my joys and sufferings, my daily cross, my life, my work, the body you have given me, my responsibilities, my concerns. Sufficient for the day thereof, I should think. Lord, help me to remember that!

32. "Pray, My Brothers and Sisters"

Bread and wine, work of human hands, have been offered in prayer by the priest. What we have made ready for the feast has been offered to God.

The priest addresses the people to dialogue with them. He wants the people to ratify his prayer with their own. He initiates an exchange about what he and we have done. We are together in this, he says: You pray too.

We pray that *our* sacrifice may be acceptable. It will be acceptable when we make it Christ's too. His was the perfect sacrifice, the sacrifice to end all other sacrifices. From now on it is a matter of keeping going and of renewing the sacrifice of Christ. All our preparation and getting ready is to join our sacrifice with his, himself with us.

We are acceptable in the measure Christ can identify with us. Our sacrifice will be acceptable in the measure it can be identified with his.

PRAYER

Lord, it is especially meaningful to me that I, with others, am offering *our* sacrifice. I join my sacrifice with yours and with others' sacrifices to make a sacrifice acceptable to God.

THE EUCHARISTIC PRAYER

33. A Hymn of Praise

The beginning of the Eucharistic Prayer is a hymn of thanks, a paean of praise. We gather up creation in a prayer to God the Father.

With this prayer we are crossing the threshold of the preliminaries into the great hall of the sacrificial feast. We have warmed ourselves at the fire; we have made friends with everyone; our hearts are in a generous spirit. We are in our Father's house and God has talked with us. We are in a mood to celebrate.

God is the Creator who has surrounded us with all good things. All of creation is a sign of God's love, the hymn of God's handiwork. His feast is a marriage feast, between lover and beloved.

We are God's people, and he is our God. Because God loved us, we are; because God loves us, we continue to be.

The priest voices our praise and thanksgiving. When he has finished we acclaim God: Holy, holy, holy!

PRAYER

Lord, forgive me for not remembering all you are and continue to be for me. You created me in my mother's womb. Indeed, even before that, I was in your mind and heart from all eternity. You preformed me, and you continue to form me, and all is good, all is holy. You made me part of God's family in the Mystical Body of Christ. Praise and thanks to you!

Our Salvation History

*(What follows is an expanded Eucharistic Prayer in an impro-
vised form, plus commentary, by way of explanation and meditation.)*

Friends and neighbors, brothers and sisters in Christ Jesus,
we have arrived at this point in our lives,
and at this point in our celebration,
through the love of God our Father and Creator.
God is our God who continually creates us anew.
Through his Son he has brought us together,
and his Spirit is present among us.

Let us begin our praise to God
by recalling how in the beginning
the Spirit of God hovered over the veil of nothingness,
and how God, by his almighty Word,
filled up the abyss with that variety
and splendor we daily see around us still.

Let us recall, too, how,
because God first loved us, we exist;
how, when after a long time, earth was ready,
and God with loving care prepared a place for us.
God brought men and women forth
out of the womb of the earth
and breathed into them the Spirit, God's Spirit.
Like unto himself, God brought them forth
in God's likeness and image.
Like unto himself, God made humankind complete,
an everlasting value.
Like unto the Trinity, God made them,
male and female he made them,
complete like God in a community of love.

God looked at what he had done and saw that it was good,
and in the cool of the evening, God walked in the garden.
For the earth, our first mother,
and for God, our first Father,
for day following night as a sign of God's faithfulness,
the name of the Lord be praised!

Father in heaven,
it is right that we should give you thanks and glory:
You alone are God, living and true.
Through all eternity you live in unapproachable light.
Source of life and goodness, you have created all things,
to fill your creatures with every blessing,
and lead all people to the joyful vision of your light.
Countless hosts of angels stand before you to do your will;
they look upon your splendor
and praise you night and day.
United with them,
and in the name of every creature under heaven,
we too praise your glory.

HOLY, HOLY, HOLY...

34. God's Mighty Deeds (Eucharistic Prayer continues)

Father, we acknowledge your greatness:
all your actions show your wisdom and love.
You formed man in your own likeness
and set him over the whole world
to serve you, his creator,
and to rule over all creatures.
Even when he disobeyed you and lost your friendship
you did not abandon him to the power of death,
but helped all men to seek and find you.
Again and again you offered a covenant to man,
and through the prophets taught him to hope for salvation.

Having made men and women, God loved them with an everlasting love.
Having made us, God never forgot us again, not one of us.
The walking God did with Adam in the garden was an everlasting walk by our side,
an enduring presence that grows more intimate
as we grow ever more human and more faithful.

From the days of Abraham when the Lord first appeared to him
and made a covenant with him, and later on dined with him
under the tree before his tent,
God moved closer to humankind.
Hand in hand they walked together now
while Abraham grew into a family, and his family into a multi-
   tude,
with signs and wonders out of Egypt, into a people God called
   his own.

Great things God did for his people down through the years;
great things God did for us who followed after in the footsteps
of patriarchs, matriarchs, prophets, and wise people of all ages.

Father, you so loved the world
that in the fullness of time you sent your only Son to be our Savior.
He was conceived through the power of the Holy Spirit,
and born of the Virgin of Mary,
a man like us in all things but sin.
To the poor he proclaimed the good news of salvation,
to prisoners, freedom,
and to those in sorrow, joy.

Not content with God being our God, and our being God's
     people,
God unfurled his plan fully
when the almighty Word "leapt " down from heaven
to become one of us, a human being like ourselves.
In him God's love for us found final focus.
In him the final age of the world is come upon us.
In Jesus, our eldest brother,
we have become sons and daughters of God.
No more merely walking in the garden together,
no more just walking hand in hand,
in Jesus we are God's children.
With Jesus we are members of the one royal household in all the
     world.
From now on we are in God's reign,
and the reign of God is within us.

PRAYER

Lord, Scripture scholars tell me that the story of your "chosen people" is also my story. How often do I forget that I am not

alone, that I have a history that links me all the way back to Abraham, and to you, my God! How often am I aware that you walk with me in my life as you did with Adam in the garden? Indeed, you continue to live your life within me!

35. The Lord's Supper (Eucharistic Prayer continues)

In fulfillment of your will
He gave himself up to death;
but by rising from the dead,
he destroyed death and restored life.
And that we might live no longer for ourselves but for him,
he sent the Holy Spirit from you, Father,
as his first gift to those who believe,
to complete his work on earth
and bring us the fullness of grace.

So that he might become the first of many brothers and sisters, Jesus sealed with his blood
our brotherhood and sisterhood with him,
our status as children of God.
He gave us a sign of this seal the day before he died,
three days before he rose again.
He gave us an enduring sign of our relationship with God
in the breaking of bread and the pouring of wine.

The Upper Room

The scene is the upper room in Jerusalem.

Jesus begins the Passover meal with a psalm of praise and thanks to the Father. The youngest member of the group — that would be John — repeats the traditional question which the Jewish boy asks his father: "What is different about this night?" Then

Jesus slowly recited the "mighty deeds" of Yahweh who guided the people out of Egypt into the Promised Land... from a land of darkness, slavery, and ignorance into a new life of freedom, united under one Lord.

As the meal progresses, they look upon — and partake — of the Passover lamb, a sign, as they would later realize, of Jesus himself.

The scene is impressive no matter how many times it is recalled.

Two thousand years later, Christians gather at the Eucharist... "eucharist" which means thanksgiving, a joyful recalling of what God has done for us and *is doing* in us:

> "Father, all-powerful and ever-living God, we do well always and everywhere to give you thanks through Jesus Christ our Lord. Through his cross and resurrection he freed us from sin and death and called us to the glory that has made us a chosen race, a royal priesthood, a holy nation, a people set apart. Everywhere we proclaim your mighty works for you have called us out of darkness into your own wonderful light."

So it is particularly appropriate — "it is right" — to give thanks and praise especially at Mass, our Passover, our Eucharist, when we remember what God is doing in us.

PRAYER

Lord, what can I do at Mass that will help me identify more and more with your sacrifice of praise? Perhaps it is as simple and as profound as saying thanks, for when I am grateful, I am ever open to receive more. The ungrateful heart expects — and receives — little. Thank you, Lord, for having called me "out of darkness into your wonderful light."

The Eucharistic Prayer Continues

He always loved those who were his own in the world.
When the time came for him to be glorified by you,
his heavenly Father,
he showed the depth of his love.

"With desire," he said,
"have I desired to eat this last meal with you before I suffer."

While they were at supper,
he took bread, said the blessing, broke the bread,
and gave it to the disciples saying:
Take this, all of you, and eat it:
this is my body which will be given up for you.

In the same way, he took the cup, filled with wine.
He gave you thanks, and giving the cup to his disciples said:
Take this, all of you, and drink from it.
This is the cup of my blood,
the blood of the new and everlasting covenant.
It will be shed for you and for all
so that sins may be forgiven.
Do this in memory of me.

36. Under This Sign

This above all is the time to believe. Even when Jesus first promised the Eucharist, to give us his flesh to eat and his blood to drink, many of his followers said: "This is a hard saying and who can listen to it?"

Many of them, Scripture relates, "turned back and walked no more with him."

This happened while he was still alive, physically in their

midst. Is it any easier to believe today when Jesus is not visibly in our midst? We have only the words of Jesus: "This is my body and my blood" and the command of Jesus: "Do this in memory of me."

In faith, we believe what we cannot see, and really cannot understand either, that under this sign made sacred by Jesus, Jesus is present to us. In faith, we believe, on Jesus' word alone, that in this sacrament the bread and wine brought up and offered are now the body and blood of Christ. With faith and thanksgiving we receive him under the sign of bread and wine and we become one with him.

The essential thing, as always, "is invisible to the eye." But, "Faith will tell us Christ is present, when our human senses fail." (From Benediction hymn: Tantum Ergo: Praestet fides supplementum sensuum defectui.)

Those who heard Jesus' proclamation mused, "How can this man give us his flesh to eat?" (Jn 6:52). "To tell the truth," our present Holy Father Benedict XVI says,

> that attitude has been repeated many times in the course of history. It would seem that, deep down, people do not want to have God so close, so available, so present in their affairs. People want Him to be great and, in a word, rather distant. They ask themselves questions to demonstrate that in fact such closeness is impossible. (At the closing Mass of the 24th Italian National Congress in Bari, on the Solemnity of Corpus Christi, May 29, 2005)

But Jesus said unequivocally: "Truly, truly, I say to you, unless you eat the flesh of the Son of man and drink his blood, you have no life in you" (Jn 6:53).

PRAYER

Lord, as I participate in the Sacrifice of the Mass, it does not seem terribly hard for me to believe that you are present, body and blood, in the Eucharist. I may have more difficulty in believing that you are present in the person next to me, or in that person across the aisle with whom I don't get along. We are all members of the Body of Christ. As with all transcendent matters, seeing is not always believing. Believing is in acting even when we don't see. I believe the person next to me, and the one across the aisle, is my brother or sister, or I don't believe!

Memorial Acclamation (Eucharistic Prayer continues)

When we eat this bread and drink this cup,
we proclaim your death, Lord Jesus,
until you come in glory.

Bread blessed and eaten, and wine blessed and drunk
are the sign of Jesus' sacrifice,
of his body broken and his blood poured out,
the sign of the new relationship of oneness
        between God and us,
between us and others.

Let us proclaim the new mystery that is ours now,
        in the new day of the Lord,
        in the days of the new relationship with God,
        and with each other:
Jesus our brother
        is Christ the Lord,
and through his Spirit,
        we are children of our Father in heaven.

37. "Let Us Proclaim the Mystery of Faith"

To "proclaim" is to declare publicly, to announce to the world, to shout it out (if we would). Like the partisan at a political rally!

Somehow in our devotional life — in our worship — we have forgotten how to proclaim... and why!

In our gathering at worship we have just recalled what God has done for us in Christ. We acknowledge his presence among us. We make it a point to dwell lovingly on what he is accomplishing among us. In the face of all the problems in our personal lives and in the world that would say nay, we assert that Christ indeed lives, risen, among us.

There is a psychology about repeating out loud, publicly, what you believe in. If you repeat it often enough, and firmly enough, you begin to grow in conviction. "Tell me what you believe in, what you hope for, and I'll tell you who you are." We are children of God and brothers and sisters of Jesus.

If there is any goodness in your life, proclaim it. If there is ignorance, or laxity, or indifference, believe that it can be overcome in Christ: "Dying you destroyed our death, rising you restored our life." Christ's living presence among us here at Mass gives more than human meaning to our striving and to the love and support we show one another.

Our personal restoration to life, and the renewal of the world, obviously is not automatically accomplished. If you want it to happen at Mass, you have to begin it in your own life. There is no shortcut to life with the risen Christ.

Yet, as we proclaim that Christ has died, is risen, and will come again, we impress it upon our consciousness. We become more aware each time of his saving power in our lives.

PRAYER

Lord, it is too much for me to think of all the good things that you have left us in the Mass all at once. Thanks for not putting such a burden on me! Yet, I can recall them one at a time... and, over time, meditation on the reminders of your goodness will naturally break out into praise. I need to proclaim your wonders!

38. The Memorial Prayer (Eucharistic Prayer continues)

Father, we now celebrate this memorial of our redemption.
We recall Christ's death, his descent among the dead,
his resurrection, and his ascension to your right hand;
and, looking forward to his coming in glory,
we offer you his body and blood,
the acceptable sacrifice
which brings salvation to the whole world.
Lord, look upon this sacrifice
which you have given to your Church;
and by your Holy Spirit, gather all who share
this bread and wine
into the one body of Christ, a living sacrifice of praise.

Let us remember this man Jesus now,
this Jesus our eldest brother in whom God was well pleased,
on whom the Spirit descended at his baptism,
this Jesus who is the first of all creation,
first fruit of those who have fallen asleep,
the first to rise from the dead,
so that in him all will come to life again,
this Jesus who is Christ the Lord,
with whom we are children of God.

Let us remember him now and never forget him,
neither today, nor tomorrow, nor forever.

So that we might remember him truly, and be more like him,
so that we might recall all that he was and is,
all that he said and did,
and fashion ourselves according to him...
so that he might teach us all things necessary,
down through the ages,
so that he might be present within us, and among us,
he promised to us the Spirit.
So that we might know him intimately,
he promised to send his Spirit upon all who asked him.

The apostles were the first upon whom he sent his Spirit,
and the Spirit transformed them into new creations.
Alive with the new life of Christ,
they worked wonders in his name.
They spoke the good news of Jesus to all who would listen,
and those on whom they laid their hands,
in turn received the Spirit.

So has it been down through the ages.
Those upon whom Jesus sends his Spirit
know him intimately and are transformed,
and, even while proclaiming the wonders,
they work wonders themselves in the name of Jesus,
the Spirit coming again and again
upon all who ask to be baptized.

39. The Mass as Memorial

The Mass is not a simple remembering, but a "memorial." Christ's life, the Last Supper, and his death on the cross are not merely called to mind, but actually become present sacramentally.

When our ancestors in the faith recalled at the Passover how God led them out of the slavery of Egypt into the desert to make a covenant with them on Mount Sinai, they were not to be simply remembering their deliverance. They knew it to be a renewal, a re-experiencing of God's great deeds in their lives, a looking forward to the fulfillment of God's covenant in the Promised Land.

So it is at Mass. In "this memorial of our redemption," we recall Jesus' death, resurrection, ascension, and sending of the Spirit, but we do not simply remember these saving events. Under the sacred signs, Jesus' sacrifice is actually renewed, our covenant is re-experienced, we are even now being saved, and we look forward to the fulfillment when Christ comes again in glory.

Calvary and the Last Supper continue to be made present at the Eucharistic assembly. We look to the past to experience it in the present and to anticipate its fullness in the future.

"Every time, then, you eat this bread and drink this cup, you proclaim the death of the Lord until he comes in glory!"

PRAYER

Lord, when I come to Mass, help me to experience what I do here, what we do together, as actually being accomplished at this moment in my life. I am not just going through the motions. I am even now being saved through the death and resurrection of your Son. Come, Holy Spirit, enlighten my mind and enkindle my spirit!

40. Commemoration (Eucharistic Prayer continues)

Lord, remember those for whom we offer this sacrifice,
especially our Pope, our bishop, and the bishops and clergy
*   everywhere.*
Remember those who take part in this offering,
those who are present here and all your people,
and all those who seek you with a sincere heart.

We pray:
Send your Spirit, Lord Jesus.
Send anew upon the world today,
upon the high and the low in all places,
send anew upon your Church today,
upon all of us who proclaim your name,
your Spirit.

Touch us as you touched the apostles
with fiery tongues and a burning desire.
Touch us as you, God, did of old
the lips of the prophet with a live coal.
Make contact with us, put your finger on us,
lay your hands upon us,
shine your face on us, transform us,
shape us to yourself, renew us in your Spirit,
for without you we do nothing.
Without your Spirit we are paupers before you,
and remember you poorly.
Without your Spirit, we know you only feebly,
as out of a book, secondhand.

Make yourself real to us, therefore,
by sending your Spirit upon us,
so that you will be in us and we in you,

so that we may at last proclaim,
each of us from the housetops:
"Finally, at long last, I live
because Jesus is the Lord,
and Christ is alive in me."

Remember those who have died in the peace of Christ
and all the dead whose faith is known to you alone.

Remembering the Christ who lives in us,
we who live in him also recall with hope in our hearts those
    who have died.

Father, in your mercy grant also to us, your children,
to enter into our heavenly inheritance
in the company of the Virgin Mary, the Mother of God,
and your apostles and saints.
Then, in your kingdom,
freed from the corruption of sin and death,
we shall sing your glory with every creature
through Christ our Lord,
through whom you give us everything that is good.

41. We Remember to Commemorate

At the Last Supper, in the close companionship of the upper room after the institution of the Eucharist, Jesus spoke of many, many things with his apostles. "You are my friends," he said to them, "I have called you friends and told you everything. My Father keep you now. Not only you, but all who will believe in me. That they may all be one, as you, Father, are in me, and I in you."

There is a tone of intimacy and of love in the long discourse in John's gospel, as Jesus commemorates the time he spent among them.

And now we call to mind, we commemorate, the passion, death, and resurrection of our friend Jesus. We call to mind and commemorate the whole happy family of Christ's friends, living and dead: his mother, the apostles, the martyrs down through the ages, the saints of all time, those trying to be his friends this very day, the entire people of God, the family gathered together before him in church, those we know and those who are in need: the poor, the sick, victims of all kinds; our brothers and sisters who have gone to their rest in the hope of rising again.

We call to mind, we commemorate, for to remember someone is already to make them present among us.

PRAYER

Lord, send me your Spirit. It is the Spirit who makes us one. It is through the Spirit that I can recall all you have done for me, and for all my brothers and sisters, living and dead. Jesus said that he would send the Spirit to enlighten us on all that he left for his apostles to proclaim. It is through your Spirit that we can continue to proclaim your gospel for all time.

CONCLUDING DOXOLOGY

Through him,
with him,
in him,
in the unity of the Holy Spirit,
all glory and honor is yours,
almighty Father,
for ever and ever.
Amen.

Through this Jesus, who is the Christ the Lord,
and through the Spirit he has sent,
God our Father be praised today and every day,
and beyond all days forever.
Amen.

42. The Mass, a Dialogue

The Mass is a conversation with God. We talk to God and God talks to us, as during the Penitential Rite and the Liturgy of the Word. The Mass is also a dialogue between priest and people.

The dialogue between priest and people is a real one; it should really be heard. That is why some of the people's parts are called "acclamations."

There are three of them during the Eucharistic Prayer, and we ought to acclaim in no uncertain terms our approval of what the priest is doing and saying.

The first of these acclamations is the "Holy, Holy, Holy" after the hymn of praise. The second is the proclamation after the consecration. It has several forms. The third is the great "Amen" at the end of the Eucharistic Prayer.

Do you approve of the very high and holy things happening before your very eyes? If you do not, what are you doing here? If you do, then let yourself be heard.

After the priest consecrates, he "shows" the bread and the cup to the people, but at the end of the Eucharistic Prayer he "lifts them up" to the Lord. Jesus said: "If I be lifted up, I shall draw all things to myself."

It is a solemn and satisfying moment. The great "Amen" is a ratifying event.

PRAYER

Lord, I want to affirm that through, with, and in Jesus, everything good in my life comes from you. Everything that is good in the world comes from you. Thank you for allowing me to experience your goodness in this Mass. Amen!

43. The Great "Amen"

The great St. Teresa once remarked that if people really knew what they were signing themselves up for when they prayed, they wouldn't do it lightly.

"Let it be!" we say. "Amen"… "Yes"… we agree completely with God's plan. We open ourselves to the full potential of God's word in us.

Ours cannot be a casual response. We are committed to more than we can imagine.

All things were made through Christ, St. John tells us. St. Paul follows with the strange statement that if anyone is in Christ, they are a "new creation." "The old creation" where people lived only for themselves has gone, and now the new one is here. It is all God's work. It was God who reconciled us to himself through Christ and "gave us the work of handing on this reconciliation."

This work is demanding. It is no less than the making of "a new heaven and a new earth." "Behold, I make all things new," says Jesus: where people no longer live for themselves.

As in baptism, in each Mass we are again plunged into Christ's death and resurrection: death to all that resists God and his plan to be realized in us, death to all that is opposed to the new community that he came to found, death to all that is not love.

And resurrection to all that is risen: love, joy, peace, patience — the fruits of the Spirit who is given to us.

At Mass we pledge ourselves to no less than the making of a new world. But we would not be able to do anything without Christ.

Christ gives us himself at Mass.

PRAYER

Lord, in the Mass we think "big." Yet, it is little by little, and bit by bit, that I say "Amen," "So be it," "Your will be done" in my life. It is only because I can proclaim from my heart, with conviction, the "Great Amen" of all time, that I can begin to say it in my time, in my day. Amen, Lord!

COMMUNION RITE

44. The Lord's Prayer

*"Let us pray with confidence to the Father
in the words our Savior gave us."*

The natural thing for us here is to stress that we pray "in the words our Savior gave us." What could be more acceptable to the Father than the very words of his Son?

But the Church very wisely also counsels us to "pray with confidence" because that is the way the Son prays. It is not only the words we say, but how we say them. The effectiveness of our prayer depends on our faith, which is really to pray with trust.

Christ prayed as a son: "Father, I know that you always hear me.... Father, everything that is yours is mine." Dare we pray that way?

"I tell you solemnly," says Jesus, "if anyone says to this mountain, 'Get up and throw yourself into the sea,' with no hesitation in his heart but believing that what he says will happen, it will be done for him." Of course, the Lord is not speaking here of moving real estate! He continues with an even more startling statement: "I tell you, therefore: everything you ask for, believe that you have it already, and it will be yours."

Believe that you have it already!

The Epistle of James, as we have seen, has something to say about how to pray and why we do not get what we pray for: Pray with faith, he says, without wavering, and do not ask wrongly, that is, for things to satisfy your unruly passions.

Do we pray that God's reign come in our lives, and in the world? It is already begun. Our daily bread? Forgiveness? Final perseverance? Help us, as you said, Lord, to believe we have it already, and it will be ours!

PRAYER

Father, I know you want me to ask, because your Son said I should. But I also know that you know my needs even before I ask, for the Spirit in me speaks for me "with sighs too deep for words."

Father, let me also know, with Jesus your Son, that you indeed always hear me and will me good, for all that you have is mine. What more could you give me than what you already have in Jesus, through whom you give us all good things?

45. "Our Father"

God, we know, is neither male nor female. Some people today have difficulty praying to God as "father." Others pray to God as "she," or "mother." Julian of Norwich spoke of God and Christ as "mother." In 1978, Pope John Paul I said in a talk that God "is a father, but even more a mother." Suffice to say, God has been revealed to us with both fatherly and motherly qualities, but God is father and mother in a wholly transcendent sense which our minds understand only faintly.

Apart from the contemporary question, however, many people may not realize how preoccupied Jesus was with talking about his Father and about revealing his Father to us.

The Father is mentioned over 250 times in the Christian Scriptures; 200 times in the gospels alone. Jesus talks about him as "my Father," "your Father," "the Father," "God the Father," and "our Father."

The Father is a New Testament revelation by Jesus. The

very few times the "Lord Father" is mentioned in the Jewish Scriptures seems almost by accident.

Jesus alone knew the Father and he talked about him endlessly. He obviously wanted very much that we know his Father and that we learn to love his Father as he did. To know him was to love him: he is all things good, true, and beautiful.

Jesus himself prayed to the Father often: "I confess to you, O Father... " "Abba, Father..." "Father, if you will, remove this chalice..." "Father, into your hands...."

That is why, if we are going to ask Jesus for a prayer and he is going to give us one, it can only begin in the one way it does: "Our Father" ... and the prayer is going to talk about our Father and us.

PRAYER

Jesus, ask your Father and ours, to give me the trust I need to respond to you as you would have me do. Help me to address your Father as "Abba, Father!" as familiar a term as when a child calls out "Daddy!" If you used that term for "your Father and my Father," we ought not to shy away from such like intimacy.

46. "Our Father Who Art in Heaven..."

How many of us when we pray the Our Father find ourselves really conscious of the words we are saying before we come to the request, "Give us this day..."? We "slip" through the first part of the Our Father, as we often do perhaps when reading or hearing the Scriptures. We know that prayer or that Scripture passage already. Or do we?

One of the startling things about the Our Father is that the first part of the prayer is all about God and God's design for us and our world. How often when we think of prayer do we think first of all about God's interests, rather than our own? Yet, if we really understood God's reality, if we truly prayed the first part of the Our Father, the second part of the prayer would take care of itself! If, for example, God's kingdom came in its fullness on the earth, all things would come with it. That perfect world, of course, will come only with the coming of Christ in glory. But we pray and work for it now, even in our own time.

Our Father who art in heaven: God is our Abba Father, and he hears us with great love and intimacy as his children, but God is still God, a mighty God, so far above everything that we can conceive of in our minds and sense with our hearts and feelings. We have no other way of thinking about our God except as Jesus reveals him to us, as nothing earthly, nothing that is not transcendent.

Hallowed be Thy name: To name God is to name the All Holy... Yahweh, whose name the people of God in the Old Covenant could not even speak! Our God is worthy of all praise, all thanksgiving, all adoration. To invoke God's attention, we need to address him with deepest awe and respect, even though God is our Father. We do not take God's name in vain. We live our lives in such a way that they become our "spiritual worship."

Thy kingdom come: Jesus came to establish the kingdom of his Father; it was his all consuming desire and task. In some sense, it is also our task. In some sense, it is here already as he said: "The kingdom of God is within you." The kingdom is also yet to come, not complete, not established in everyone all over the world and in the world itself. In spite of the kingdom's exalted nature, it is to be — with God — our prime goal on this earth. Do not our concerns, at times, seem rather petty in comparison?

Thy will be done: Obedience to the will of God in our lives and in the world has been revealed in God's word and by the saints and spiritual masters throughout time as *the* reason for our existence. To have God's will, which is really his love, as the desire of our hearts is the only way to happiness in this life and eternal life in the next.

On earth as it is in heaven: In heaven everything and everybody is perfect. We will fully know what this means only when we reach it. Now we can only pray that the kingdom come in all its fullness even now, when all people will treat themselves, others, and the created universe with respect and love for the salvation of the world.

Give us this day our daily bread: We ask for food and sustenance not only for our bodies but also food for the soul, for our minds, hearts, spirits. That comes from the "daily bread" of the Word and the Eucharist. Christ is the "bread from heaven," and he comes to us in a tangible way in the Mass.

And forgive us as we forgive those who trespass against us: As we have noted in the Introductory Rites, we cannot have it both ways: If we are to expect God's forgiveness, we need to forgive ourselves and our neighbors, even those who have hurt us.

And lead us not into temptation: God does not tempt anyone, the Scriptures tell us, but we have "the world, the flesh, and the devil," enough to contend with! God allows temptation to come to test us (not for God's sake, but for our own self-knowledge). We need to know who and what we are and to seek God's help and salvation.

But deliver us from evil: God in Jesus is the only one who can "deliver" us; Jesus is our Savior; we do not save ourselves. How many times have we asked for his help and have experienced his deliverance?

In the liturgy of the Mass, the Church, ever conscious of our needs, gives a further inspired reflection on the final request of the Our Father:

Deliver us, Lord, from every evil, and grant us peace in our day. In your mercy keep us free from sin and protect us from all anxiety as we wait in joyful hope for the coming of our Savior, Jesus Christ.

PRAYER

Jesus, may your kingdom reign in my heart and in my life — in my whole spiritual formation field. Help me to understand that if I truly pray and live the Lord's Prayer, I will be able to conclude with full heart: "For Thine is the kingdom, the power, and the glory, now and for ever. Amen."

47. Prayer as Jesus Taught Us

Jesus, who is the way, the truth, and the life, said simply, "Pray *in this way*: Our Father...." Our marvelous Christian tradition, expanding on the nature and practice of prayer, has informed us and, more importantly, *formed* us in the many ways of prayer — all more or less simple.

"In him (Jesus Christ)," says St. Paul, "we live and move and have our being." This is a firm foundation for our experience of prayer in the Christian tradition. In our prayer life — inner prayer and vocal, private and communal, we give form to that awesome truth.

"Behold I am with you always," Jesus says. "The Holy Spirit [when you are in trouble] will give you words to say." In our prayer we "connect" with the Holy Trinity who lives within us by grace as baptized Christians. And in our prayer life we connect with one another in the Body of Christ — particularly in the Mass, but also in family prayer, and as we pray for and with one another.

The Church's liturgical year, the liturgies of the daily Mass and *The Christian Prayer of the Church* (the Liturgy of the Hours) lead us into reflection and meditation on Christ's birth, his home life at Nazareth, his public life, his great passion-sacrifice-death on the cross, his glorious resurrection, and the sending of his Spirit. Our imitation and following of Christ in his life ushers us into his and the Father's awesome life and love.

— How he suffered and died for each one of us personally can give us strength and courage when we meet our own crosses in life.

— His love shown in his words and life can wound us so we become more vulnerable to his life and appreciative of this most real of realities.

— We know that we can bring our own problems and challenges to the foot of Jesus' cross and believe and trust that somehow in some way our prayer is heard and answered.

How the Saints Prayed

The saints and mystics have given us time-tested maxims:

— St. Paul assures us that the Holy Spirit prays within us "Abba (that is, Father)" with signs too deep for words.

— Prayer, says St. Teresa of Avila, is simply being in the presence of God and conversing with One who we know loves us.

— According to long Christian tradition, prayer is "the lifting of the mind and heart to God."

— Thomas Merton wrote that prayer is simply being before God, longing to do his will.

— St. Paul says: "Offer yourselves as a living sacrifice of praise, wholly acceptable to God, your spiritual worship."

— John Cassian advises "unceasing prayer," nourished over a lifetime by *lectio divina*, particularly meditation on the

Psalms. His favorite: "O God, come to my assistance; O Lord make haste to help me!"
— St. Paul says, "Whether you eat or drink, or whatsoever else you do, do all for the glory of God." "Pray always," he adds.
— Then there is, finally, silent prayer: contemplation, the prayer of simple presence, the Jesus Prayer, Centering Prayer.

Of course, most of us do not come to these "simple" ways of praying easily. It may take a lifetime of effort and surrender to God's loving guidance. A trusted way to nourish our prayer life is "formative [not primarily informative] spiritual reading." This is a reflective, meditative pondering over a trusted text to lead us to pray in Jesus and in the Spirit. This slowed-down "reading" for forming our characters, nourishes us in four ancient prayer methods:

— *lectio divina* (holy reading), the prayerful reading of a passage of Scripture, a story or a parable.
— *meditatio* (meditation), a silent interior reflection on what has just been read.
— *oratio* (prayer), a response which results in a prayer, dialogue or spiritual journal entry.
— *contemplatio* (contemplation), a resting in the word, in which the word sinks from head to heart.

Modern sentiment adds a fifth method implied by the ancients:
— *actio* (action), the result of prayer leading to inspired action.

48. Sign of Peace

"Let us offer each other a sign of peace."

There is much talk of peace, and this at a time when there has never been more division: between husbands and wives, parents and children, liberals and conservatives, hawks and doves, nations and nations. Yet, Christ came to heal divisions: between God and human beings and between human beings themselves.

We come to Mass to be reconciled... and to be reconcilers.

But we can deceive ourselves. We cannot come to Mass with hates stored up inside and expect a few gestures to disgorge them. Divisions are not healed without anguish, as Christ's sacrifice was not accomplished without the cross.

Christ did not come to bring a false peace: "Do not suppose that I have come to bring peace to the earth: it is not peace I have come to bring, but a sword."

The "sword" of Christ is not a sword of dissension so much as a sword of values, the priority of truth. What Christ is, and what he stands for, causes divisions in our world because everyone is not equally for the truth, and where there is no meeting of hearts in Christ there can be no peace. (But when people meet in Christ, there is peace despite differences.)

There is a further cause of hate and division: We fight against the "dark forces" in us, against "principalities and powers," against Satan, the prince of division.

Fortunately, we have a Lord who is stronger than all the forces of evil. "Peace, I bequeath to you," he said, "my own peace I give you, a peace the world cannot give.... Do not let your hearts be troubled or afraid."

PRAYER

Lord, give me the peace that only you can give. Help me to set my priorities, get my life in order, so that my heart and mind can rest in you. I know deep peace can come to me only when I am conforming my life to the image implanted in me. Do not let my association with anything or anybody lead to a deformation of that image. And don't let that happen to all the other troubled people either!

49. Sign of Love

"We've come a long way," someone said, speaking of the sign of peace. "The other evening, our pastor explained that the Mass was supposed to be 'a gathering of people who love the Lord and one another, are grateful that he died for us, who come together to enjoy a meal with him — a sacred one — to share their joy and their trials, to pray for strength, give thanks, and go out into the world better able to cope.'

"We might want to show our joy, by smiling at each other as we go to the table and return. We ought to feel relaxed and comfortable because we are friends and the Lord is our friend.... And it is beyond me to hear Americans who have such a variety of ways to greet each other, say they don't know what to do at the greeting of peace. Do whatever is most comfortable and natural, but do greet one another with love in the name of the Lord."

PRAYER

Lord, some people are more able to greet one another than me, others less. Let me not judge anyone, but also let me not be stingy with my gesture of peace. If I really am at peace, it will show, more or less, despite outward appearance. Let me mean it when I say, "Peace be with you." If I am not at peace, may my gesture of peace to my neighbor bless both of us with the peace you alone can give.

50. Lamb of God

At Mass we recognize Christ as the Lamb of God who was slain. We hail him as the only human being on earth who became so deeply involved with our guilty condition that he became, in St. Paul's words, sin.

To be a Christian — to be present at Mass — means to be willing also to take on the sins of the world, as Christ did, and to be a savior with him.

The sins of the world! It is a sad discovery for every one of us as we grow older that life is one long discovery of evil in the world, or so it seems. We discover that there are such disorders as sins of the world with which we cannot cope, and which carry us along like a torrent, moments of evil that take us in, and which except for the Lamb of God would have the upper hand.

Happily, we are not called upon to solve the problem of the world's evil. Christ did not solve the problem of evil, of sin, of guilt. He took it upon himself. To be a Christian is to do likewise.

We begin to be saviors with Christ when we realize that we are somehow involved in the sin, the guilt, of the world. Most of us are willing to recognize our obvious personal sins; we are less willing to admit to consciousness those that are less obvious and that constitute our share in the sins of the world. Many of us rarely come to the realization that our sins extend beyond ourselves and our immediate surroundings. Because of that we can never be saviors.

But there have always been people who were willing to be so: perhaps the spouse of an alcoholic, a parent of a teenage drug addict, a person dying of cancer, survivors of oppression who wait patiently, who refuse to hate.

Dutch spiritual writer Huub Oosterhuis put it well: "Whenever this strength — we call it forgiveness — is visible, the fatality of evil is broken and the world is justified. Such people are greater than sin. They do not solve the problem of guilt. But, in their lives, they bear it away. They are the people who take away the sins of the world." They are those who have made themselves one with the Savior.

PRAYER

Lord, am I willing to suffer, to take on the sins of the world with you? Do I, with St. Paul, help to make up "what is wanting" in your sacrifice? That is an awesome thought, Lord, that my salvation, and that of others, is somehow dependent upon my participation in the cross. I do want to be with you in everything, even in the cross I both dread and desire.

51. Breaking of the Bread

It is one of the most delightful stories in Scripture, how those two disciples on their way to Emmaus were taken in by the stranger, and the stranger allowed them to be taken in by him.

The two were sad because Jesus had been crucified. And the stranger asked them: "Did not the Christ have to suffer?" He expounded the Scriptures to them to prove it. When they arrived at Emmaus they invited the stranger in because it was already late by then. At supper they recognized the stranger "in the breaking of the bread," and with that the risen Jesus was gone from them.

"Did not our hearts burn within us when he was talking with us?" They did indeed. There is a happy ending to the story of Jesus: he is risen, he is among us!

The bread at Mass is broken as Christ was broken for the sins of the world.

The bread is broken while the Lamb of God is asked to take away the sins of the world.

The bread is broken so that we may share in it.

It is a rich moment at Mass. It is a point of convergence in which memorial, meal, and sacrifice come together and can all be seen at once, when Christ's dying for the sins of the world, our remembering, and our sharing Christ, crucified and risen, are all there together.

PRAYER

Lord, am I willing to be broken as the bread is broken, as Jesus was broken, so that others may recognize you in me? Help me to recognize you in the broken of this world, in those who do not show your beauty or your strength in outward appearance, but bear only the features of the crucified. Help me to recognize you in the broken in me and in those around me here at Mass.

52. "Lord, I Am Not Worthy"

What shall we say when the Lord calls us to his supper? We came to celebrate with him and each other that Jesus is Lord. We have stood, waited, prayed, and gotten ourselves ready, singly and together, and now we are called to be happy together at his supper.

Spontaneously we answer: "Lord, I am not worthy... but...." But what? But, yes, of course, if you want me to. But, yes, of course, if you will say the word. The fact is, he has already said the word: Come, come, do come....

That's part of what makes us worthy even when we say we aren't. We aren't and we are. The less worthy we are, the more God wants us to come. We are worthy because out of love God created us. We are worthy because out of love Jesus died for us. "I came to save sinners," he said. Come, you sinners. The bigger the sinner that is saved, the more God has done for them, the more they are worthy.

We aren't worthy — except that we are. We are his from the beginning, right down through the middle, and to the end of our lives because Jesus has purchased us with his love and his life. We are even called his people. How could we be anybody else's? We are not on the outside looking in. We are on the inside, happy to be at home with him.

PRAYER

Lord, "worthy" is derived from a Latin word meaning "having weight." I must have great weight because you carried me on the cross and you paid a great price for me. How could I be so ungrateful as not to come and receive your gift? Lord, make me more and more aware, and worthy, of your unconditional love for me.

53. "Only Say the Word..."

No one is worthy to stand before God. It is a fact that is quite obvious. The Lord just takes it for granted: "If you who are sinners know how to give your children good things...."

What is important is not our unworthiness (although we need to acknowledge that) but our faith and trust: "Only say the word and I shall be healed."

There was the centurion in Matthew's gospel whose servant was lying at home paralyzed, and in great pain. When Jesus said he would come and cure him, the centurion replied: "Sir, I am not worthy to have you under my roof; just give the word and my servant will be cured."

Matthew continues: "When Jesus heard this, he was astonished and said to those following him, 'I tell you solemnly, nowhere in Israel have I found faith like this.'"

When faith is strong it works wonders. When it's not there, James tells us in his epistle, we needn't expect anything. Not because God withholds his power from the unbelieving and untrusting, but because we need to trust and abandon ourselves. Only when we learn to rely no longer on our own strength, our own plans, are we able to open ourselves to the power and guiding word of God in whom we believe.

Without faith and trust, life ceases to have meaning. With faith and trust, we see wonders all around.

PRAYER

Lord, I trust in you because I am becoming more aware of your love and mercy in my life. I trust that, if I continue in your love, everything in my life works to my good. On looking back on my life, I am more and more convinced that I have experienced that truth. Thank you for your healing presence.

HOLY COMMUNION

54. To the Father:

Father, your kindness is beyond words:
You have gathered us together in Jesus.
You have forgiven us in his name.
    We have reconciled ourselves to our brothers and sisters
    so that we may ourselves be forgiven.
"You have fed us with your Word.
Now you feed us with your Son:
    Bread to share with one another,
    wine to gladden our hearts together."

(*Eucharistic Liturgies*)

To the Son:

Your memory we keep, O Lord.
Especially those last moments
when you spoke with such loving urgency:
    "Do not let your hearts be troubled...."
    "I shall not be with you much longer...."
    "My commandment is that you love one another...."

    "I shall not call you servants any more."
    "I shall call you my friends."
    "You are my friends, if you do what I command you."

    "One can have no greater love
        than to lay down his life for his friends."

    You have been lifted up, O Lord;
        now draw all things to yourself.

To the Holy Spirit:

Now we know how good it is that Jesus went away,
for we have his Spirit of love among us.
The Spirit —
 who makes us cry "Abba Father,"
 who teaches us in our hearts,
 who breathes into us new life,
 who makes us springs of "living water,"
 to live as a people in peace and love.
Indeed, he did not leave us orphans.
Come, O Holy Spirit, Come!

55. "I Have Longed and Longed..."

"With desire have I desired to eat this Pasch with you before I die."
"I have greatly desired to eat this Passover with you...."
"I have longed to eat this Passover...."
"I have longed and longed to share this paschal meal with you...."
These are the words of Jesus, variously translated, as he sat down to his last supper with his apostles.
This was no ordinary meal for Jesus. This is no ordinary meal for us.
For Jesus it was the meal before he suffered, before he died. For Jesus it was the meal he had waited for to share with his friends; it was the meal on which he would heap special significance, his sacrifice, special love, special power. It was the meal that would never end.
It is meant to be the same for us: strength before we go out and suffer for others, a meal steeped in significance, a meal

shared with friends, a meal marking our identity with Jesus, a meal binding the Christ in all of us together in communion and community, a pledge of everlasting life.

The bread is our sign. "The body of Christ," the priest says.

And each of us says "Amen" to that, knowing that the bread is the sign of the body given to us for our life together.

Let anyone who can say "Amen" to the bread and to "the body of Christ" come forward now, eat and be friends, be happy, be joyful, be healed, be grateful, be warm with love, and celebrate in the heart of Christ.

PRAYER

Lord, when I think of your desire, your longing, to be with me, I am ashamed at my lack of longing. Yet, I do desire you. You are my heart's desire. You put that desire there, that longing, that restlessness. Thank you for that restlessness, and may it increase!

CONCLUDING RITE

56. The Blessing

"Blessing" is a good-bye word, a word that comes to us from "God be with you."

It is a most common thing among us to part with a blessing in our hearts for one another, and in our hearts we know that all blessing comes from God. To bless is to believe in God.

While all blessings do, indeed, come from God, we are God's instruments in blessing — the people of God in a special way. All who are baptized into the priesthood of Christ, all who believe in God, are the instruments of blessing.

That priests bless the people in God's name, and that parents ask the blessing of God on their children, and that we bless one another, has a long history and precedent.

That Christians bless one another and all the world is the message of Jesus. We are sent on our way with the blessing of God to bring the good news to all that in Jesus we are all blessed. We are to be a blessing to others.

PRAYER

Lord, sometimes "blessed" in Scripture is translated "happy," or "fortunate." I am indeed blessed at Mass, and I am happy when you bless me there. Help me to experience the truth of your beatitudes when you say, "Happy are the poor in spirit... those who mourn... the clean of heart... those who thirst for justice." With that spirit, I can also be a blessing to others.

57. Blessings in the Bible

We read early in the Bible that when God first created man and woman, he blessed them.

God blessed Abraham when he sent him into a new country. Moreover, God promised to bless those whom Abraham would bless.

In a significant event, Melchisedech, "priest of the most high God," brought out bread and wine and blessed Abraham en route on his journey.

Abraham blessed Isaac, and Isaac blessed Jacob, and Jacob blessed his sons.

In a very strange story, Jacob, on leaving Laban and preparing to meet Esau, wrestled all night with an "angel," and even though his hip was dislocated in the struggle, he would not let go until he had wrested a blessing from God.

Tobias blessed the marriage of his son to Sarah in the phrase still used: "The God of Abraham, the God of Isaac, and the God of Jacob be with you."

Jesus blessed the loaves and fishes that he multiplied for the crowd.

When the little children came to him, Jesus put his arms around them and blessed them before they went away again.

At the Last Supper Jesus blessed the bread and wine, the night before he died, leaving it for a sign of himself after his going away.

In a final gesture of love, Jesus lifted up his hands and blessed his disciples as he departed from them at the ascension.

All these blessings were occasioned by situations involving departures of one kind or another.

We are blessed, and are a blessing to others, as we depart from Mass.

PRAYER

Lord, how it must have felt to be in your presence when you gave a blessing! Yet, you are blessing us all the time. It is at Mass that we are especially aware of it, when we are blessed, and are a blessing to others in return.

IV
The Way of Contemplative Presence in the World

DISMISSAL

58. "Go, Live the Mass"

Our Mass is not finished with a few gestures.

The Mass is a sign and a revelation of what is actually taking place in our own lives and in the life of the community, or it may be only an empty ritual or a jumble of sounds.

We have heard God's Word and eaten the Bread of Life. Now it is time for us to leave, to do good, to praise and bless the Lord in our daily lives.

It is easy enough to say; we have heard it hundreds of times: "Go, to love and serve God and one another." Do we allow its full meaning to penetrate our awareness?

As one spiritual writer put it: In the Mass we have seen God at work in human life, a God who loves us so much that he took thousands of years to break gently into the life of the world, and actually become a human being to be among us. He became a servant, humble, gentle, poor, with the good news that our God is a God who loves us, who forgives, who is everlastingly concerned for our welfare.

At Mass we are summoned and commissioned to continue that revelation of God's loving action in the lives of humanity and the world by repeating his gestures of love, sharing, forgiving.

We have no better place to start than in our own homes, among the members of our own families.

Every time we share a meal, then, give thanks, recall God's mercies, forgive each other's faults, we carry on the Eucharist, the Mass, where we remember and imitate him who chose to love us "even to death on the cross."

That is the burden and the privilege we bear.

PRAYER

Lord Jesus, help me to understand that all my life is sacramental, as you in your lifetime were the great sacrament of God. You are the sign and symbol of God's loving kindness, and we are a sign of your goodness continuing in the world. I want to be a small light in that sign.

59. Being Sent

We are leaving. We are leaving the place made sacred by our coming together for worship, made sacred by being set aside as the ritual meeting place of humanity with the mystery of God, a special place for rendezvous between God and us.

Almost everything we did there, and said there, was a sign — from putting our host in the cup to sharing in Christ's body and blood in communion — a sacred sign putting us in touch with a world that we cannot touch and see, a world more important than the world we can lay our hands on.

The world of God is the world of mystery and world of spirit. What is most human about us is spirit and mystery; what we seek to become and what we yearn for in our deepest heart is hidden and invisible.

The whole effort, activity, and significance of what humanity calls religion is to make contact and keep contact with the mystery of God, with the Spirit of love at the heart of humanity.

We are leaving, but we are not *just* leaving. We are being sent away, out of this sacred place into the world in which, if Jesus' coming to us means anything, it means our going out as he did to express the mystery of God and to keep alive the Spirit of love in ourselves and among others in the world.

Pope Benedict expresses the proper spirit of today's Catholic as he or she leaves Sunday Mass. Quoting the early Christians, he says,

> "We cannot live without meeting on Sunday to celebrate the Eucharist." That was the early Christians' answer when asked why they celebrated the Eucharist, even when threatened by death to not do so.

Just like the early Christians, Pope Benedict continues, without the Eucharist, "We would not have the strength to face daily difficulties and not succumb."

Pope Benedict gives wise advice: "It is not easy for us... to live as Christians. From a spiritual point of view, the world in which we find ourselves, often characterized by rampant consumerism, religious indifference, secularism closed to transcendence, might seem such a harsh wilderness.... We need this bread [the Eucharist] to cope with the toil and exhaustion of the journey." (Pope Benedict's homily at the closing Mass of the 24th Italian National Congress in Bari, on the Solemnity of Corpus Christi, May 29, 2005.)

Go, and live the Mass!

PRAYER

Lord, I truly believe I am being sent on a mission, to be your ambassador of love and service to your people. Thank you for allowing me to experience a little of your Spirit for the life of the world.

60. "Contemplative Presence"

Once when Jesus was in the house of his friends Mary and Martha, he confronted Martha about her excessive solicitude about the work of hospitality and her complaint about her sister, "who sat at Jesus' feet." "Martha," he chided, "you are busy about many things. Only one thing is necessary. Mary has chosen the better part."

What Jesus reproved in Martha was not her attempt to make her guests comfortable but her failure to integrate her action with the contemplation that was its source. "It was not because of her work — it was good and holy — but because she was overly concerned," writes a noted early 14th century spiritual master. His recommendation follows:

> We must perform good and useful work, in whatever way it comes to us; the care, however, should be left to God. We ought to do our work meticulously, silently, and with inward recollection. With such a disposition we shall draw God into it, for the eyes of our soul will be turned inward, devoutly, and lovingly.
>
> And always we should examine our motives and rectify our intentions. We must listen to the Holy Spirit, whether he prompts us to rest or to work, and then be faithful to his prompting. If he wishes us to rest, let us rest; it he wishes us to work, then let us do it with good cheer.[14]

If only we could learn that!

How do we maintain the contemplative spirit? Father van

---

[14] Johannes Tauler, *Sermons* 47, p. 155, quoted by Muto and van Kaam, the Epiphany Association ELFA '99 Workbook, p. 91.

Kaam suggests that we Christians in the world today might be "in danger of losing our spiritual inspiration and transcendent strength" if we would dispense with the sacraments, especially the Mass, "or to neglect to imbibe meditatively their deeper meaning."[15] Is that not what we have been trying to say?

Van Kaam cites a pervading kind of "self-alienation" in our modern society. It is that sometimes experience of not feeling "at home" in our world at large, in our country, community, or neighborhood. There is a deeper and more positive meaning, van Kaam asserts. It comes, he says, in a spiritual sense of alienation, the core of which is a "loss of at-home-ness," a spiritual self-alienation that comes from a spiritual questioning of myself, of the spiritual dimension of my life, and the "mystery" of my life's direction by God — a definite function of the more contemplative spirit.

Specifically related to the Holy Sacrifice of the Mass, van Kaam points out that the stages or parts of the Mass correspond well to the stages in the process of self-alienation and self-emergence of the Christian in the world. In the Mass, as we have seen, the celebration of our death and resurrection with Christ is central. If we are alert and reflective, we may view our own process of "self-alienation and self-emergence" in the death of our old self and the rising of the new self. When we hear the mission to "Go and live the Mass," we emerge, repentant, reconfirmed in our following of Christ, and united with him and our brothers and sisters.

The Mass is a way of formation, reformation, and transformation: of dying with Christ, becoming more like him as we

---

[15] Adrian van Kaam, *Dynamics of Spiritual Self Direction*, Epiphany Books, Pittsburgh, PA, 1992, p. 189. This and the following analysis is from Chapter 7, "Self Direction and Self Alienation."

assent to the offering of ourselves, and are confirmed in that new life in union and communion.

The *first* stage or way of formation expressed in the liturgy of the Mass — the Introductory Rites, the initial rites of purification and confession of sins — is our remorseful and sorrowful "alienation" from our old self.

The *second* way, that of reformation, is "reflecting on the new self to be born," its emergence expressed in the Liturgy of the Word, the homily, and the creed.

The *third* way, the way of transformation, the offering of our sacrifice with Christ's sacrifice is expressed (1) in the offertory, the "death of the old current self and transformation into a new current self more in tune with God's will for me at this moment of my life," and (2) in the consecration and communion — the Liturgy of the Eucharist — my experience of union with Jesus.

At the dismissal of the Mass, I am sent back into the world with this "contemplative presence," "the incorporation of my new or growing current self into the community of the faithful and of my sisters and brothers in the secular world."[16] It is the final stage of the Mass when our prayers of peace and communion result in a better self emerging "to love and serve God and neighbor."

PRAYER

Lord, teach me what kind of "presence" I now have in my family, my relationships, my work, and my world. I must admit that it is not always as signified by my presence at Mass. Let me learn and live the Mass!

---

[16] Ibid., p. 190.

61. The Christian Presence in Society

People in every age can point to the angry, violent, and corrupt nature of their particular society. Ours is no exception. It is into just such a world, however, that Jesus sends us as "sheep among wolves." If we look at our situation in a positive, Christian manner, it can be seen as a challenge and a privilege to follow and imitate Christ in sorrow and joy.

What is the Christian "social presence"? With many Christians seemingly caught up in the same kind of social and un-Christian ambitions and attitudes which guide our materialistic and achievement-oriented society, it would seem that some of us haven't a clue as to the answer to that question. We do not sense the erosion of our higher ideals and aspirations that comes along with the depletion of effective Christian social concern. Our idealism fades quickly in the heat of the secular battle.

When the Christian's social presence is founded on "contemplative presence," however, it can become effective even though not explicitly noticed, or averted to. People who have this presence, which we maintain should be the result of our faithful participation in the Mass, have been gifted with the "grace of social inspiration, of a deepening of the theological virtues of faith, hope, and love in the service of Christian social presence."[17] That keeps them detached from the control, dominance, and striving for instant success that bring on the "deforming D's" — the dissonance, denial, depletion, disillusionment, and discouragement — often affecting the Christian in the world today.

---

[17] Van Kaam, *The Dictionary of Human and Christian Personality Formation,* quoted in *Epiphany International,* 1998.

PRAYER

Lord, keep me from a misplaced pride in my own accomplishments acquired by my attempts to control my own destiny, often at the expense of others. Save me from the selfish, nerve-wracking striving that drives me to that control, and ends with my own dissipation and discouragement. Give me that peace that comes from reflecting on your care and concern for me and my loved ones.

62. Contemplation

Contemplation is what we have been leading up to, not the contemplation of the exotic, mystical experience, but the "active contemplation" of the Christian in the world who lives by faith, trust, and love in reflection and prayerful concern.

As noted, God wants us to live lives of harmony (consonance), of peace and joy. The Christian who has the contemplative vision sees, however dimly, the presence and action of God in the routine of his day, in the lives of people, events, and things of his everyday experience. That Christian, nourished at the table of the Eucharist, sees in a sense God in all things and all things in God, as the saints have told us. This vision is the result of the Christian's experience of the awe of the Creator in the things God has made, things in their deepest meaning. Contemplation is what guides us in this deep seeing of all things in tune with God's vision.

Probably there are very few older priests and religious who have not sometime in their training come across a spiritual classic that might be considered somewhat out of date today. That classic, *The Soul of the Apostolate*, by Dom Jean-Baptiste Chautard, O.C.S.O., published nearly a century ago, documents in no uncertain (and sometimes rather harsh) terms, that unless our outward action proceeds from an inner inspiration of a heart in union with Christ, it is doomed to fail in its purpose and be spiritually ineffective and even damaging. Our contemplative, prayerful attendance at Mass should result in the integration of contemplation and action — a key trait of Christian character formation. How do we practice this integration in our lives, this essential "Mary and Martha" rhythm of worship and work, leisure and labor, prayer and participation?

The spiritual journey also demands a serious and strenuous concentration on the study and practice of the spiritual life — spiritual reading, reflection, prayer, meditation, contemplation. It demands a "contemplative presence" for anyone who would live a spiritual life or, even more, guide others on their own spiritual journey.

Prayer

Lord, you know my on-again, off-again history of attending to my spiritual journey with you. Help me to remember that my Christian presence in my family, society, and world today depends upon my relationship with you. Let me find in my prayer at Mass and in my private prayers as well the inspiration and graces I need to be Christ to others.

63. Justice, Peace, Mercy

Active contemplation nourished by our Christian revelation, tradition and doctrine, as we have suggested, allows us in a certain sense to see all things, people, and events as God sees them. It appreciates them "as divinely inspired pathways to awe-filled presence in and with Christ and to the Trinity dwelling within and without us." "The presence of the Most High," van

Kaam continues, "can be contemplated in all events, people, and things in cosmos and nature. Such contemplation bears fruit, among other things, in care for our surroundings and in works of justice, peace, and mercy for all."[18]

It is at this juncture, as we are being sent out on a mission for Christ, that we are urged to practice "the works of justice, peace, and mercy for all." This is the way of contemplative presence and action. Here we echo back to a consideration of the C's of Consonance we reflected on when discussing how to listen to the word of God at Mass and its meaning in our lives.

Recall that peace and joy in our lives can come only from our conformity with God's will for our lives as planned from all eternity. It presumes that we are always discovering our life call, to be fully disclosed only over a lifetime. The more this conformity becomes a reality in our lives the more harmonious they become, the more consonant, "sounding together with" the music God wants to play on our human instruments. Recall the four C's of congeniality, compatibility, compassion, and competence. These are conditions for the possibility of manifesting genuine, Christlike care in our relationships and in our world.

Congeniality

Congeniality, that sense of "at-home-ness" with ourselves, others, and our situation in life, means that we respect the original, unrepeatable uniqueness of self and others. "We strive gently and firmly to nurture our own and their unique-communal call in Christ-like care. Our ability to say yes to the gift that we are may be enhanced when others who really care say yes to us. They offer us confirmation of our true originality in God. Such confirmation must extend not only to those near and dear, but,

---

[18] Ibid., 1997.

as Jesus made clear, to anyone who comes within our circle of care."[19]

Compassion

To be a person of compassion full of care "implies that we remain sensitive to our own vulnerability and human limitations, as well as those of others. We are called to bear with one another and to show loving concern, to understand and forgive. Such compassionate care does not emanate from ourselves alone. It is a gift made possible only in Jesus through the power of the Holy Spirit."[20]

To be a competent person "is to be willing to grow continually in the wisdom, knowledge, and skills given to us by God so that we can be most effective in our formation field. To be epiphanic manifestations of divine love in the world, we must hear and obey the words of Jesus, *Go out and bear fruit, fruit that will last.* We must point others toward the 'More Than' for which we all hunger and thirst, while remembering that we are only servants through whom others might come to believe."

Courage

"To competently implement congenial, compatible, and compassionate care requires courage. Courage enables us to persevere, to press on toward the goal of becoming spiritually mature in Christ so that we may mirror the Mystery of peace and joy for which all creation longs."[21]

It may happen, as in many lives, that living in this harmo-

---

[19] Muto and van Kaam, *Becoming Spiritually Mature*, Formation Guide, p. 141.
[20] Ibid., p. 142.
[21] Ibid., p. 143.

nious kind of existence seems to be out of the question because of home and family situations, uncongenial life work, difficult and complex relationships, etc. Living in "contemplative presence" does not necessarily mean life without trouble; it does mean a serious attempt to live in some kind of attentive silence, reflection, and abiding in God's providential care for us. Living the Mass can help us to do just that.

PRAYER

Lord, you know the deepest desires of my heart. If I were truly in tune with the desires you place there, I would know that in your will is my peace and joy, for you will only what is best for me. Help me to live in harmony with the music of my being in you.

PRAYER

Thank you, Lord, for this new day
in which you call me to be an Epiphany
of your care and concern.
Radiate your presence through me
in my family,
in my place of labor
and leisure.
Give me the grace to meet you in the sacrament of everydayness.
Let me share in the beauty of your hidden life in Nazareth.
When I fail, let me experience in joy your forgiveness
in which I am immersed always, everywhere.
Teach me to turn obstacles and failures,
benefits and successes
into formation opportunities.
Strengthen my commitment to be a manifestation
of your love and tender mercy.
Amen.

Composed by Father Adrian van Kaam
for the Epiphany Association

ST PAULS

This book was produced by ST PAULS/Alba House, the Society of St. Paul, an international religious congregation of priests and brothers dedicated to serving the Church through the communications media.

For information regarding this and associated ministries of the Pauline Family of Congregations, write to the Vocation Director, Society of St. Paul, 2187 Victory Blvd., Staten Island, New York 10314-6603. Phone (718) 982-5709; or E-mail: vocation@stpauls.us or check our internet site, www.vocationoffice.org